Life Matters

David B. Whitlock

Life Matters

David B. Whitlock

Parson's Porch Books

Life Matters

ISBN: Softcover 978-1-936912-58-2

Copyright © 2012 by David B. Whitlock.

All rights reserved. No part of this book may be reproduced or transmitted in any form or by any means, electronic or mechanical, including photocopying, recording, or by any information storage and retrieval system, without permission in writing from the publisher.

Unless otherwise noted, all Scripture quotations are taken from the *Holy Bible*, New Living Translation, copyright 1996, 2004. Used by permission of Tyndale House Publishers, Inc. Carol Stream, Illinois 60188

Scripture quotations marked "NIV" are taken from THE HOLY BIBLE, NEW INTERNATIONAL VERSION, copyright 1973, 1978, 1984 by International Bible Society. Used by permission of Zondervan Publishing House. All rights reserved. The "NIV" and "New International Version" trademarks are registered in the United States Patent and Trademark Office by International Bible Society. Use of either trademark requires permission of International Bible Society.

To order additional copies of this book, contact:

Parson's Porch Books

1-423-475-7308

www.parsonsporchbooks.com

Parsons Porch Books is an imprint of Parson's Porch & Company (PP&C) in Cleveland, Tennessee. PP&C is an innovative non-profit organization which raises money by publishing books of noted authors, representing all genres. All donations from contributors and profits from publishing are shared with the poor.

This book is dedicated to the readers,
the ones who actually pick up a newspaper and read it.

Table of Contents

Preface	9
Chapter One: The Seasons of Life Matter	13
Chapter Two: Marriage Matters	31
Chapter Three: Parenting Matters	48
Chapter Four: Mom and Dad Matter	63
Chapter Five: Death Matters	78
Chapter Six: The Holidays Matter	95
Chapter Seven: Tragedies Matter	116
Chapter Eight: Celebrating Life Matters	129
Chapter Nine: Life Lessons Matter	143
Chapter Ten: Sports Matter	163
Chapter Eleven: The News Matters	177
Chapter Twelve: Becoming your Better Self Matters	194

Preface

"One thing about him, when he was there, he was all there."

I was listening to Dr. Gibson Winter, then Professor for Christianity and Society at Princeton Theological Seminary. Dr. Winter had this wonderful way of sharing an aside--an "oh by the way" story--which would invariably have a meaning all to itself, staying in my mind long after the words of the lecture had been snuffed out by the stuffy air of Stuart Hall.

On this particular occasion, he was describing a colleague, whose name I've forgotten. The man, the subject of Dr. Winter's anecdote, was notorious for getting so immersed in his work that he would on occasion be a tad late for a faculty meeting or even his own lecture. He was the proverbial absent-minded professor: almost at times comical, yet respected and beloved. Upon arriving, he would light up the room, engaging others in lively conversation, making it easy for them to overlook his occasional tardiness.

Then Dr. Winter capsulated his description of his colleague in that one phrase: "When he was there, he was all there."

I could visualize this man; indeed, I felt as though I already knew him. You know him or her, too. These rare individuals are all there when they are there.

They are the ones you wait on at the theater, or save a seat for at the restaurant, or strain your neck for as you anxiously anticipate their arrival at the ball game. "Where could he be?" you ask. "Do you think she remembered the address?" you wonder. "Did he get so immersed in his research that he forgot our engagement?" you question.

And you want this person to be there.

I could see Dr. Winter's friend arriving with disheveled hair, wearing in his tweed coat, wrinkled shirt, and blue jeans. He opens his arms wide to embrace his friends, apologizes for being late, and smiles as he asks how they are. And he means it.

And suddenly everyone's little measure of agitation evaporates as they grin in return. He's there now, all there. Wherever this person is, he lives that moment to the fullest. And like moths attracted to light, people naturally drift in his direction.

I've often wanted to be more like that man, whoever he was. Unfortunately, I haven't always been all there, once I was there. Too often I've been distracted by the place I had come from or the people I would see next. I've brought the problems of the past into the present or pre-played the worries of the future into the now. And in short, I wasn't there.

I've learned, ever so slowly, little by little, that life is lived in the moment, or it isn't lived at all; if I'm not here, I'm either in the past--which is no more--or I'm in the future, which is not yet. If I'm still wandering around in the hallways of the past, lost in a maze of regret, or trying to catapult myself from the present into the next time zone, which can't be entered until it arrives, it's not simply that I'm not here: I'm actually *nowhere*.

Like T.S. Eliot's J. Alfred Prufrock--lingering on the outside looking in, fearful of the present, doubting, wondering, questioning whether he has "the strength to force the moment to its crises?" anxiously awaiting the future, mistakenly believing that, "There will be time, there will be time/To prepare a face to meet the faces that you meet"--we miss the thrill and excitement, victories and defeats, struggles and accomplishments of the present when we aren't fully alive in the moment, willing to risk ourselves in it.

Life matters in all is variegated aspects. It must be grasped, breathed, and lived for all it is now: "This is the day the Lord has made, we will rejoice and be glad in it" (Psalm 118:24), the Psalmist proclaimed. And Jesus warned, "Don't worry about tomorrow, for tomorrow will bring its own worries" (Matthew 6:34).

I hope these essays will help you as you read them as much as they did me as I wrote them to see how much life matters, how important it is to live each moment to its fullest, and how precious is every breath we take. My desire is that you will enjoy what you read and that in itself will be part of life's gift for you.

And me, too.

These essays were printed as a self-syndicated column in newspapers in Kentucky and Oklahoma. I am most grateful to the editor of the Lebanon Enterprise, in Lebanon, Ky., Ms. Stevie Lowery, for first asking me to write for that paper. She has been a source of encouragement in the challenging task of writing. Ben Sheroan at the News Enterprise in Elizabethtown, Ky. has helped me along the way as well. My wife, Lori, patiently reads my column each week before I send it to the editors. She has a good sense of what will and won't communicate to the readers. My daughter, Mary, has given invaluable suggestions for my weekly columns. She has grown accustomed to receiving her dad's weekly email in her inbox with the subject "column." As I organized the column into book form, my son, Dave, helped with editing.

And so, with you, Dr. Gibson Winter's friend, whoever you are, O Captain my Captain, we declare with you: "Carpe Diem, make your life extraordinary." We knew you would finally arrive, at last. Have a seat and stay awhile, for after all, you know how life matters.

And now that you are here, we are all here with you.

.

Chapter One

The Seasons of Life Matter

Stuck in an Elevator--**January 2, 2010**

I never dreamed I would be stuck on an elevator, but there I was, sitting on the floor, my only companion the darkness surrounding me.

Just a few minutes before the nurses helping my wife in post-op had sent me to get my car and park it at the back entrance of the surgical clinic so that they wouldn't have to wheel Lori across a parking lot. The only problem was that I didn't wait for their directions. I dashed off like a knight in shining armor rescuing his sleeping damsel from a burning castle.

Bolting through the first door, I paid no attention to the fact that the waiting room I jogged through was empty--no patients, no nurses, no receptionists, not even a light remained on at 5:30 p.m., but that didn't matter to a man on a mission; that door and the second leading to the stairwell hardly broke my stride to the final glass door, the exit. It clanged shut, stopping me cold in my purpose-driven tracks. Not to be deterred, I quickly decided to retrace my steps back to post-op and obediently listen for further instructions.

That wasn't an option. The doors would open only from the side I came through, not the entry side.

I was trapped on the far side of the surgical clinic.

And my wife was waiting, half conscious, in post-op on the other side.

Some people have aversions to elevators. For me that elevator on the first floor of the clinic posed no threat; it looked like an opportunity, an escape route from the locked doors. So I stepped in. The elevator doors shut. Then, the power shut down, and I found myself in total darkness.

I was stuck on an elevator.

People who have studied these situations have found that the sense of panic usually subsides after about 30-60 minutes. I was on the verge of hyperventilating, just thinking that I might be there that long or even longer. How would anyone know where I was? What would my wife do? I could almost hear the nurses' conversation later that night, before going home: "Hey, whatever happened to that guy who went for his car? He just vanished. Too bad we had to call social services to get his poor, abandoned wife."

I'm reminded now, as I reflect on how helplessly I sat on that elevator floor, of how we romp and stomp through life, dashing through doors that lock shut behind us, running the red lights, barreling down the road to success like a fast train through a ghost town at midnight, virtually unaware of the hollowness that haunts us as we hurry down the track, deafened by the roar of our own steam, racing by moments we can never retrieve-- moments that are the life of life: the kids running into the bedroom with morning kisses, the baseball accidentally crashing through the picture window, the ballet recital, the romantic candlelight dinner, the quiet moments by the fireplace.

And quite suddenly the doors shut, like the lid on a casket, as we sit motionless in our own elevator, pink slip in our hand, entombed in mediocrity, plateaued in an aimless career, temporarily laid off, or unavoidably reassigned; or perhaps it's a trapped relationship with one who doesn't care enough to shrug his shoulders, stay, or leave. And we can't help but ask, "Was it my fault? Was this necessary? Was it just fate?" We wait, and hope for the foreman, or plant manager, or Someone (Where did He go?) to bring us better news.

He may not arrive on our time, but He is there on time, always. Faith ultimately overcomes fear; determination overpowers doubt when faith and hope rest in the right Someone.

And then my elevator quite suddenly moved. The doors opened. Light streamed in. I laughed. An angel-nurse laughed back. "It's a good thing I came this way, pushed the elevator button, by chance."

By chance? Not on your life. I knew better.

Senior Coffee, Anyone?--April 3, 2010

Where were you when you first recognized you were getting older?

We remember where we were for other significant moments, don't we? I remember, for instance, where I was when I learned that President Kennedy has been assassinated: Ms. Speck's second grade class room at Washington Elementary School, Altus, Oklahoma. I recall where I was when the Challenger went down: in my apartment in Louisville, Kentucky, working on a seminar paper for my doctoral requirements; and 9/11: driving down Prien Lake Road, Lake Charles, Louisiana, listening to the radio, intrigued by the unusual news about a plane crashing into the World Trade Center. We remember where we were when those significant nation-altering events occurred.

But, what about getting older? Do you perchance remember where you were when you first realized that was happening? Were you at the optometrist office and learned you needed bifocals? Was it on your own driveway when your child outran you to the street? Or was at the pharmacy as you ordered cholesterol medication? Or was it at the college campus for your child's orientation?

For me, it was a fast-food restaurant. I was on my way to a lunch meeting with my oldest daughter. Feeling drowsy, I stopped along the way for coffee in Danville, Kentucky. And then it happened: like Rip Van Winkle, I slumbered into a time warp, a twilight zone of somnambulation, and before I could process what was happening, I was at the order counter.

I requested a small cup of coffee. Simple enough. To my surprise, the young man at the counter said, "$.55." I was thinking, "This is a good deal, $.55 for a cup of coffee. It must be on sale." I stepped aside to receive my order, and then I heard the server announce in a voice loud enough to travel to Cincinnati, "SENIOR COFFEE!"

"Senior coffee?" I thought, "Me? You don't mean me, do you?" I looked to my right and to my left. No senior guy to pick up this coffee. I had heard correctly. Like Socrates taking the hemlock, I stoically, without objecting, took the coffee. "Senior Coffee," I mused, "surely not me; surely not yet." But there it was in my hand, my coffee, my Senior Coffee.

The worst part was that the young man who took my order didn't bother to ask. He assumed I was a senior. He didn't say, "I know you're probably much younger, and excuse my ignorance in asking such a young looking man as you, but I'm required to ask, so, do you get the Senior Citizen Discount?" No, it was as if I walked into that restaurant, suddenly grew a grey beard, donned an "I've been everywhere" traveling cap, put in a pair of hearing aids, and ordered my coffee, my Senior Coffee.

I stood there, slack-jawed, not knowing whether to give the coffee back, explaining that this was a case of mistaken identity, offering to pay the regular price for a small cup of coffee, laughing at the naiveté of the young man who took the order---a youngster who obviously couldn't tell that I can do a hundred push-ups, run on my elliptical trainer for thirty minutes, work ten hours a day, and most obviously, (can't you see?!) quite obviously--a young man who couldn't manage to recognize that I have a full eight months, (that's 240 days or 5,760 hours) before I am considered by any standard a senior citizen!

In a split second, I decided to leave it alone. It didn't matter. I smiled and walked away, sipping my coffee, my Senior Coffee.

And to my surprise, I liked the flavor.

So then, fully awake, I could see it clearly: I'll take the senior coffee... savor each sip...and enjoy the life, old as I am.

Life Matters

Your Retirement Day May be Nearer than You Think--June 24, 2010

"Am I ready for retirement?"

I asked myself that question last week at my dad's retirement reception. Of course I'm not ready for retirement. Unless someone drops a couple of million into my bank account, it will be years before that day arrives in my life. But, preparation for retirement begins long before actual retirement. The question, "Am I ready for retirement?" has to be asked with a measure of urgency, and the sooner the better. In a sense, we have to get in the retirement mode, which is difficult for most of us. Someone said it like this: "When you retire, think and act as if you were still working; when you're still working, think and act a bit as if you were already retired."

When we fail to plan for retirement we plan to fail in retirement. This past year millions of Americans awoke on their retirement day with some sobering news: apart from either government assistance or family support, they do not have the resources to survive their retirement years, much less enjoy the fruit of their labor. For thousands, this is the direct result of the 2009 financial collapse; for others, simple negligence is the cause.

The truth is, less than half (43%) of Americans have calculated how much they will need to retire. I've learned it's much more than I thought. One reason it will take more than many anticipated is because of the simple fact that we are living longer. The average life expectancy in the US was 72.6 years in 1975; by 2007, it had increased to 77.9. For many people who will live into their 80s, 90s, and even 100s, this means they will be retired longer than they worked, says Carl Macko, CFP, president of Synergy Capital in Smyrna, Georgia.

But there are other reasons, according to Forbes.com reporter Lisa LaMotta. Adult children can have money problems, which can quickly drain the parents' financial resources. In addition, health care costs and taxes, inflation, and home repairs are all potential problems just waiting to absorb your retirement fund. Financial advisors, I hasten to add, strongly recommend not touching retirement savings to address these unexpected situations.

But, the question still remains, "Am I ready for retirement?" Let's suppose I did win the lottery, and won millions. Would I be ready for retirement? We can have all our financial "ducks in a row" and still be "sitting ducks," unprepared for what awaits us. Our inner lives will not suddenly be different at retirement than now. A good retirement begins with a good today.

Each today leads to another tomorrow; each day is filled with whatever we choose to put into it, which is the condition for what we receive from it. How we live each passing moment will bear the fruit we will eat in later years.

The day after Dad's retirement reception, Dad, my two brothers and I, met for coffee. I couldn't help but overhear a worker say at mid-morning break, "I just can't wait for this day to be over." I understand, I've had days like that. But then again, I wondered if that was her life, one can't wait to get it over day at a time.

The retirement reception for Dad was outstanding. My sister-in-law, Joy, had been there to make it happen. All I had to do was show up, and then at the close, help Dad up the steps. It was there, holding his hand, that I caught his smile again, and as he glanced my way with that smile, it was quite suddenly early Saturday morning, December, 1962.

I could feel my dad's steady hand lifting me into the air between steps as my seven year old feet, striving to keep in step with his fast pace, were lifted by the strength of his arm. Hurrying alongside Dad, left hand warm in my coat pocket, right hand secure in his, I was afraid of missing the moment, in this case, arriving at Art's Boot Shop before he closed at noon, anxious as I was for a new pair of Christmas cowboy boots. And in that moment, looking up at Dad, I felt his smile, as he too anticipated what lay ahead.

Now on this day, 45 years later, as I slow my walk to match his hobbled, uncertain ones, I embrace that same smile, grasping the adventure of walking together. Retirement day is only the culmination and continuation of life's crooked, meandering, and thrilling uphill climb. The walk is as much the adventure as the arrival. And retirement is just another step in the mystery of this life we live, even as it reminds us of our boundaries, our limitations, and our expiration date.

The Days Go By--March 21, 2011

It's a line from the Eagles 1975 classic hit, Tequila Sunrise: "The days go by."

And they do. Whether you like it or not, whether you waiting for (or enduring) a tequila sunrise on a beach in Acapulco, or working in a coal mine in eastern Kentucky, or trading stocks on Wall Street, or writing songs in Nashville--the days go by. Like wet sand slipping through our fingers, the days go by.

Lori and I have a friend who takes old videos and transfers them into a DVD. People give him their wedding ceremony, children's birthday parties, anniversaries, and other significant life events. The quality on the DVD is better and more enduring.

So Lori has been going through all our family videos to see which ones we want our friend to convert onto DVD. The other night after dinner, she asked me, "Want to watch some of the family videos?"

Two and a half hours later, teary-eyed and smiling, we turned off the VCR. I went to bed, thinking that was the last of our family viewing. But the next morning, instead of the news in the background of our get-ready-for-work routine, Lori was playing another family video. "Look at that, would you?" she chuckled while putting on her make-up, pointing to then three year old Madi's recitation of the Pledge of Allegiance.

That evening when I arrived home, there was Lori again, glued to the TV, video in, on the road to becoming a family video junkie--this time watching the then young Dr. Whitlock preaching. "Wow!" she exclaimed. "Your preaching style has changed. You used to be sooo loud, and you preached FOREVER!" I think it was a compliment, but all I could see was a fuller head of hair, no gray--and smoother skin on my more youthful face.

We are a blended family, so our family video viewing takes twice as long. There was Mary-Elizabeth dancing, Harrison being awakened on Christmas day by the kisses of Skittles, his new puppy, Madi with her baby dolls, and Dave playing in his Davy Crocket outfit. Grandparents, aunts, uncles, brothers, sisters--they were all there, through all those years.

The days go by: Mary-Elizabeth gave up ballet long ago; Madi's baby dolls are somewhere; Harrison and I buried his Christmas day puppy, by then the grizzled Skittles, several years ago; And it's been years since I could hold tiny Davey high above my head--balancing him in one hand, the toddler sucking on his pacifier, kicking his chubby legs, giggling uncontrollably--and proclaim while laughing with him, "Behold, the child!"

Each moment was a moment, caught in time, pictured on camera, fleeting ever so easily, always so quickly, passing through time--time, the common denominator that levels us all until we are all equal, everyone of us--- dust.

But not dust in the wind, floating along random like, drifting in the currents of time, without meaning or purpose. Seeing years compressed in minute segmented videos reminds us of our two inescapable boundaries: birth and death. But as long as we travel, we can and should sing because we have hope of a forever life that endures beyond the family movie. As Moses said it in his prayer, "Satisfy us each morning with your unfailing love so we may sing for joy to the end of our lives."

Yes, Moses, to the end of our lives, to a life that extends beyond them. William Faulkner put it like this in his 1950 Nobel Prize speech, "I believe that man will not merely endure: he will prevail. He is immortal, not because he alone among the creatures has an inexhaustible voice, but because he has a soul, a spirit capable of compassion and sacrifice and endurance."

Maybe, just maybe, Don Henley and Glenn Frey--sipping straight tequila, waiting on the sunrise--were somehow, somewhere deep within themselves hoping for hope, thinking that there must be more, more than what is here, more than simply what we see, watching, as "the days go by."

Time Changes--March 21, 2011

Daylight saving time (DST) -- how's that working for you?

Apparently it's not so good for many of us. According to a study at the University of Alabama at Birmingham, DST may not be the best thing for our health, since it comes as such a jolt to our cardiovascular systems.

Have you been dragging out of bed since March 13, the date we moved our clocks forward this year? It's worth it, isn't it? After all, we do get that extra hour of daylight. Well, that extra hour of afternoon sunshine is associated with a 10% increase in the risk of having a heart attack on the Monday and Tuesday after moving the clocks forward, according to Martin Young, Ph.D., Professor of Cardiovascular Disease at UAB. The opposite occurs in the fall when we move the clocks back; there is a 10% decrease in risk of heart attacks.

Why the potential for harm in moving the clocks forward? One theory, Dr. Young says, is that each cell in our body has something like an internal clock that allows it to anticipate change. When there is an abrupt change-- like springing forward one hour--the cells don't have time to readjust, creating stress, resulting in a detrimental effect on the body.

Maybe that's why there is a higher incidence of traffic accidents and work place injuries on the first Monday and Tuesday after moving our clocks forward.

So, here I am, almost two weeks into this time change, and I'm still groping for that lost hour of sleep, dragging myself to the coffee pot at 5:30 a.m., reminding myself--with every heavy, burdensome, languid step--that it's really 4:30 a.m., at least according to the circadian rhythms of those cells in my body, which obviously haven't had time to readjust to this barbaric method of enjoying an extra hour of afternoon sunlight.

I feel like Bill Murray as the character Bob Wiley in the film, *What about Bob?* Bob awakens himself each morning by repeating the words in his half-awake state, "I feel good, I feel great, I feel wonderful... I feel good, I feel great, I feel wonderful... I feel good, I feel great, I feel wonderful..." I'm with you, Bob; it's just that the internal clocks in my cells haven't gotten the message yet.

It should remind us that as slippery as time is, we are still subject to it. Even something as small as a one hour time change can throw our systems into confusion for days, even weeks. Last Sunday, one of the persons who meets regularly for prayer was absent. Seeing her later in the morning, she simply explained, "Time change. I'll get used to about the time it changes again."

I understand. I get that.

Time. That's all it is, after all. And time in its essence is well nigh impossible for us to grasp. Who after all invented time? God? Not necessarily, at least according to Stephen Hawking. In his book, *A Short History of Time*, he states, "So long as the universe had a beginning, we could suppose it had a creator. But if the universe is really completely self-contained, having no boundary or edge, it would have neither beginning nor end: it would simply be. What place then, for a creator?"

Other scientists have proposed a mulitverse— a theory that describes the continuous formation of universes through the collapse of giant stars and the formation of black holes. And physicists Paul Steinhardt and Neil Turok have postulated a model where two universes collide to produce a new beginning for the universe. Time changes; it reaches back and forward beyond time, meta-time.

I still want to leave room for God in his universe, even though I have difficulty articulating the concept of time. That's why I'm with St. Augustine, who believed in God as the creator of the heavens and the earth and of time itself. But when he tried to explain time, he too was at a loss for words, "What then is time? I know what it is. If I wish to explain it to him who asks, I do not know."

Wiping the sleep from my eyes, shuffling toward the coffee pot, I know time not as a theory to be explained but as a drag on both hemispheres of my brain.

One little hour reminds me of my weakness, my vulnerability, my dependency on the One who cared enough to enter into what he created-- our little time zone here on this terrestrial ball, our little moment in time-- and deliver us from it, awakening us to more, even as we make our way through the daily routine.

Even through, God help us, Daylight Savings Time.

Till Alzheimer's Do Us Part?--September 21, 2011

When I first heard Reverend Pat Robertson's comment, I thought of Ronald Reagan's response to incumbent President Jimmy Carter during the 1980 presidential debate, "There you go again."

"There you go again, Pat," I thought. But Robertson wasn't in a debate, he was responding to a caller on his television program, "The 700 Club." This is not the first time Robertson's statements have placed him in the center of controversy. In 2010 he blamed the earthquake in Haiti on a pact he said the Haitians made with the Devil 200 years ago.

This time he was counseling a man wanting to know how to advise a friend whose wife was so deep into dementia that she no longer recognized him. The man's wife as he once knew her was gone, and now he was seeing another woman.

"I know it sounds cruel, but if he's going to do something, he should divorce her and start all over again -- but make sure she has custodial care and somebody looking after her," Robertson said.
But what about the vow, "til death do us part?"

Alzheimer's is a "kind of death," a "walking death," according to him.

Robertson was overlooking the fact that while in many cases caregivers do form relationships with others, few seek to divorce their spouse, and in fact, Alzheimer's frequently brings families closer together. Robertson was obviously thinking of the caregiver more than the patient.

Neurologist James E. Galvin, director of the dementia clinic of New York University's Langone Medical Center, said in an interview with the New York Times that victims of this horrible disease still tend to recognize those people who have been closest to them. And Susan Galeas, CEO of the Alzheimer's Association of Southern California, observes that even as victims of the disease progress toward the end stage of the illness, they are still individuals nonetheless, benefitting from loving relationships, enjoying a rich history filled with personal experiences.

Robertson was clearly struggling with the issue. He advised his listener, "Get some ethicist besides me to give you the answer, because I recognize the dilemma, and the last thing I would do is condemn you for taking that kind of action."

Robertson's comments, as misapplied as they may be, should push us to think about this issue. Rather than simply pulling the, "Thou shall not divorce card," and condemning everyone taking that route, perhaps we would do better to recall Jesus' "new commandment," the one about loving each other, the one that says "Just as I have loved you, you should love each other" (John 13:34), and ask ourselves how love is expressed for both care givers and patients in the grip of this grim disease.

More of us will be facing this unfortunate dilemma. An estimated 5.4 million Americans have Alzheimer's disease, and with the number of baby boomers soon entering their senior years, that figure is bound to increase. Nearly half the people over the age of 85 already have Alzheimer's. It's the sixth leading cause of death in the United States. It has no cause, no treatment, and no cure.

My conversations with my Alzheimer's friend move in the same circular fashion: Her mind malfunctions like a record hopelessly getting stuck in the same place, returning to the same beginning. "Now who are you?" she asks for the third time in 10 minutes. I remind her again; she answers the same: "Oh, yes, I know who you are."

Her eyes fill with tears as she remembers her deceased husband's love. And then having remembered him, she forgets him.

"How old am I?" When I remind her, she frowns as she reflects, "I just didn't know people lived that long. I can't figure out why God let me live this long, too long."

"The church, your church still loves you," I say, trying to reassure her of her place with our community.

In an instant, her frown disappears; a smile spreads across her face as her eyes brighten. "The church," she says as if an old friend has walked into the room, "the church, I've always loved the church, I still love the church."

Instead of thinking of reasons to go on without them, maybe we should look for reasons to go on with them, for when all the memories have slipped away, the love of relationships remains, and even when the present is only a fuzzy haze, they may still feel love, a love as familiar as a well worn glove, often tenderly received even when they can't remember the face or the hands that give it.

Eight letters: the space between their world and mine--May 15, 2012

Recognizing that the space between her world and the one she is slowly but surely entering is drawing closer, Pat Summitt, who has won more basketball games than anyone in NCAA history, stepped down as coach of the Tennessee Lady Vols last week. Summitt was diagnosed with early onset dementia last year, at the age of 58.

Early onset dementia attacks people younger than 65. Many are in their 40s and 50s, and some even in their 30s.

Alzheimer's disease, a form of dementia, affects millions. The statistics are staggering: According to the Alzheimer's Association, in 2011, 5.4 million Americans were living with Alzheimer's; 15,000,000 caregivers provide 17 billion hours of unpaid care at home; Alzheimer's costs the nation $200 billion annually, and someone develops the disease every 68 seconds.

If all the Alzheimer's patients were placed in one state, it would be the 5th largest in our nation.

It is predicted that if a cure for dementia is not found by 2050, 16 million Americans will have some form of the disease, with Alzheimer's being the most prevalent.

Life is by no means over with a dementia diagnosis. Like any good coach, Pat Summitt has a strategy to stay healthy as she faces Alzheimer's. And her son, Tyler, also a basketball coach, reminds us that we can learn from those with Alzheimer's. "Despite (it), she has stuck to her principles and stayed strong in her faith. Her confidence to be open about this disease has taught me the importance of honesty," he said in an interview with Carol Steinberg of the Alzheimer's Foundation of America.

Tyler is right: Victims of this disease still have much to teach us. Entering their world on a fairly regular basis, I learn from them.

And every time I look into their eyes, I'm reminded that the space between their world and mine is only the length of that eight letter word: dementia.

One, whose blank stare appears fixated on the other side of the room, no longer recognizes me.

Only several years ago he was in the early days of retirement. I remember him then, still robust, vigorous, and active. And today, I miss that wry, almost cocky smile of his.

"We love you," I remind him.

"You're a good man," he says in a monotone voice with no facial expression. I wonder if his answer is a standard response he learned years ago, like "hello," "good-bye," "how do you do?"

Stepping into the world of another, I ask this former leader in our church, "How are you doing?"

Without fail he answers the same: "Can't complain."

"Looks like you just finished eating. What did you have?"

Like a little boy who has been asked a question above his years of comprehension, he doesn't attempt to formulate a response but innocently looks to his wife for the answer.

Down the hall, I step into the world of another whose life changed years ago.

Walking her to the dining hall, she surprises me. Instead of the same question she normally repeats over and over, "Where am I?" this time she asks instead, "Who put me here?"

Not sure of the answer and not wanting to agitate her with a guess, I appeal to the highest source possible: "The Lord," I instantly tell her, masking my hesitation.

"The Lord," she says, repeating it back to me, seemingly satisfied with my response, at least for another evaporating moment in her life, and then slowly, deliberately she declares, "Yes," like a math student who has just discovered the answer to an algebraic equation that became suddenly obvious.

Walking out of their world, I get in my car, and as I turn the ignition, I ponder how the space between their world and mine is encompassed by the same love of the One who has us both in his caring hands.

In *10 Gospel Promises for Later Life*, Dr. Jane Marie Thibault tells about a nurse's answer to a dementia patient's question, "Honey, what's my name?"

After the nurse told her, the patient said, "Oh, that's right! Half the time I don't even know who I am!" Then, pointing to a cross on the wall, she said confidently, "But he does, and that's all that counts!"

Indeed it is, no matter which side of that space you are living in.

One way to save a life--June 13, 2012

He was always getting up a game of some kind, usually sandlot football.

Mark had a knack for gathering my friends and me, most of us ten years his younger, for a game of football in the fall or baseball in the spring. And he was my own personal trainer, throwing me thousands of football passes or hitting me countless groundballs, trying to make me better.

But there was more to it than the game--something much larger than that. The sport was only an avenue enabling Mark to do something far more important than catching or throwing a ball.

Before Mark made our front yard a football field or a baseball diamond, I spent most of my time with Dougie, my brother, only 18 months older than me. We were so attached as constant companions that Momma usually spoke our names as one: "Dougie and Davey, Davey and Dougie."

Until quite suddenly on a fateful day in May, after a car wreck involving the two of us and my oldest brother, Lowell, Dougie's short life was taken.

And after that, it was only "Davey."

Mark gradually emerged as our neighborhood coach and my personal instructor in all things athletic. Because of him, I dreamed big dreams and learned to work with others.

Mark even arranged for one of his high school football buddies to form a rival football team from another neighborhood so we could play them, which we did, giving Mark his first win as a football coach.

So, I really wasn't surprised when Mark announced his intention of getting his college degree in elementary education. After all, he was a natural, as was his wife, Joy, who graduated with him, both of them earning bachelors and then masters degrees in their fields. With their mutual love for kids and one another, it seemed likely that if they didn't achieve great success, they would at least have a joyful journey.

They got both.

And some forty years later--seven as a coach and teacher and thirty-three as a principal, Mark, along with a banquet room full of teachers whose lives he had touched, gave his retirement speech.

He didn't mention that along the way, he received the prestigious Academic Achievement Award from the State Department of Education, nor that he was named the District Administrator of the Year by the Oklahoma Association of Elementary School Principals in 1995 and 2009, nor that he was the recipient of the Oklahoma School Administrator Award in 1998-1999.

Neither did he mention that his wife, Joy, was named Teacher of the Year from Rivers Elementary in 1993-94 and also in 2010-11, nor did he say that Joy was a grant recipient for Award Reading from the Rural Oklahoma Foundation in 2007.

All those awards weren't really that important to Mark and Joy. What mattered was that they considered themselves privileged to invest their lives in students and teachers.

But Mark did remember to thank the teachers for their role in his journey, and when he was done, they thanked him. There was the teacher who once worked in the school cafeteria and because of Mark's encouragement, went for it, getting her degree in education and a job at Mark's school; and then there was the teacher who finally got a chance to prove herself, because Mark was willing to hire her; and another teacher had lacked confidence but gained it from Mark's support; and some, like my wife, Lori, pursued careers in education simply because of Mark and Joy's positive example of what it is to be a teacher--educators who make a difference in others and in so doing, save some students from potential disaster, pointing them to the right path in life.

I couldn't help but think--as teachers and friends gathered around Mark to thank him for caring enough to lead and teach those many years--how Mark had helped save another life, that of the skinny, six- year old I once was, the child who was lost without his brother. It was then that Mark stepped in and took up the slack, and in so doing helped save not just one life, but potentially many more as well, because he had learned the importance of instilling in others the hope that comes from dreaming dreams and the thrill that comes in fulfilling them en route to becoming whole and well.

And forty years down the road, that's still one way to save a life.

Chapter Two

Marriage Matters

Looking for a Valentine's Smile--February 15, 2010

My wife wouldn't smile Valentine's Day.

It wasn't that she didn't want to smile. She had a surgical procedure to remove a basil cell skin cancer just above her upper lip. The procedure was outpatient, not lengthy, and considered low in risk. The first stage was the removal of the cancer itself by physician number one; the second step was reconstructive surgery by surgeon number two. All went well, but as warned, a painful recovery time was part of the anticipated routine. Saturday and Sunday after Friday's surgery would be particularly uncomfortable. Eating was difficult, talking hurt, smiling out of the question. A romantic Valentine's Day would wait for another year.

Partly to ease the absence of our Valentine's weekend, I was determined at least to get her a card. Quickly shuffling through the Valentine section of cards while waiting for her prescriptions to be filled, I almost instantly chanced upon the one I wanted. It spoke to the occasion: "My Wife: All the beauty in the world is in your smile."

I hurried to the cashier, anxious to get back to the surgical clinic before Lori was out of surgery. I waited in line, behind only one person, a young lady who placed an arsenal of cosmetics on the counter. The cashier was an older woman, who seemed unperturbed, even philosophical, in responding to the young lady's questions about the kind of make-up she was purchasing. "You young people seem so intent on looking just right," she commented to the youthful buyer, "and you just don't know how beautiful you really are." The cashier seemed like the kind of person who paid attention to people, so I paid attention to her.

Then it was my turn. I handed her the card. She rang it up. "That will be $7.43," she said.

"$7.43. Dang! That's expensive," I muttered to myself. "Ma'am, I didn't realize that card was that much. Could you do a return, and let me get another?"

"Sure, I can do that," our sage cashier responded, "but first let me ask you a question." I sensed the prophetess was about to ask me something the answer of which might perhaps reveal the future, or disclose something about myself or life that I was unaware of. "Does the card say what you want it to say to your Valentine?" she asked.

"Well, yes," I hesitatingly responded, "as a matter of fact, it does. She is having surgery at this moment, and won't be able to smile for a while, and this card has a line about a smile, and I thought it might be some little thing that would make her feel better, and it is Valentine's Day Sunday, you know," I blurted out, telling her more than I had intended.

"Then," she said, "if it says what you want it to say, it will speak to her heart, and she will smile, she will smile."

And so the purchase was made.

On Valentine's Day, I gave Lori the card. "My Wife: All the beauty of the world is in your smile."

She tried to smile, but couldn't.

Most smiles are obvious; they are written on the face. Some smiles are hidden. To see them you have to look deeper, into the heart.

I looked for the smile deep within and said, "No need to smile."

No need, indeed.

Questions Women Ask--January 24, 2011

"Do you remember the color of that sweater I gave you when I was a sophomore in high school?" my wife nonchalantly asked me. "You remember, don't you? It was the first real gift I ever gave a guy. I was so proud of that."

We had been admiring the sweater our daughter had given me for Christmas. I stroked the sweater as my mind raced back 30 plus years, trying to remember and think of a proper response to her question. I could hear Ulysses Everett McGill (George Clooney) whispering in my ear the same words he spoke to his endangered companions in the film, *O Brother Where Art Thou*, "We're in a tight spot!"

Trying to avoid hurting her feelings and at the same time wanting to appear as her romantic repository of cherished memories, I struggled between confessing my ignorance and rolling the dice to guess the color. The color of the sweater our daughter had given me was brown; perhaps the odds were in favor of brown for the sophomore sweater. But then again, maybe it was the crew neck collar that reminded Lori of her love gift.

Fumbling for the right words, I sputtered; I stalled; I stammered: "It had a crew neck just like this one, didn't it?" I asked, still holding the new Christmas sweater in my hands and hoping my question would spin our conversation in another direction. No such luck was mine. "Oh, yeah, it did," she responded. "But you don't remember the color, do you?"

Now her cards were on the table. But it was possible I could recover with a royal flush by coolly expressing my surprise at her question. "Of course I remember, you silly," I could say. "It was brown, just like this one I got for Christmas. Do you really think I would forget the first gift you ever gave me? C'mon now!"

But if it weren't brown--be it any other color--my bluff would be called, the truth would out and my royal flush would morph into a pair of clubs. And I would be emotionally indebted for days, weeks, months, who knows--maybe years.

And so there I was--the cowardly gambler, beads of sweat forming on my brow, my lips quivering, all the time thinking, Lord, why do women ask such questions? Why does it matter to them? And, how do they remember these things?

Men--we are different. John Gray underscored what most of us knew in his best seller, *Men are from Mars, Women are from Venus*. "Without an understanding that men and women are supposed to be different, it is such a temptation to think that men shouldn't be 'that way' or women shouldn't react 'that way,'" Gray wrote in the introduction of his book.

Since then, Walt Larimore, M.D., and his wife Barb, have co-authored, *His Brain, Her Brain*, that documents their thesis that, "there is ample scientific evidence that supports the fact that many of the dramatic differences between his brain and her brain are inborn." In other words, there is no unisex brain. We are wired differently in areas that include sight, hearing, taste, smell, and touch. So, there was a difference in how we saw that sweater. "Rod-shaped cells (rods) on the retina are photoreceptors for black and white, while cone-shaped cells (cones) handle color. Women have a greater proportion of cones than men. So women can see colors better than men," the Larimore's point out. No wonder Lori could recall the color of that brown sweater when I couldn't!

But the biology didn't matter in that moment. I couldn't say, "Oh, Lori, you remember the color of that sweater because you have more rod-shaped cells on your retina and poor pitiful me, I have fewer to act as photoreceptors on my retina, and therefore, compared to you, I virtually see in black and white. Silly girl, did you really expect me to remember the color of that sweater?"

No, even if science were on my side, I had to come clean, and so I folded, "I'm trying to pull that up, but I just can't recall. Tell me about it."

And she joyfully did. It was from the Surrey Shop, where I used to work in high school. And yes, it was a brown crew neck.

And to think my hunch had been right all along.

"And by the way," she continued, "you do remember what you gave me that Christmas, don't you?"

Okay, Ulysses Everett McGill: time for your line again, "We're in a tight spot!"

Just One Word--February 2, 2011

All it took for Doris Troy was, "Just One Look," in the words of the hit song she wrote and sang to the top of the charts in 1963. "Just one look/ That's all it took, yeah /Just one look." Good and right for her.

But sometimes, in other situations, all it takes is just one word--one word to change a life forever.

We--my wife Lori and I--waited for that one word, having been told we would receive the results of Lori's biopsy between 2 p.m. and 4 p.m., Thursday last week. Actually we had been waiting for over a week, including the time for the scheduling of the biopsy itself and the determination of the results.

Waiting can be an unnerving experience: the human mind is capable of a thousand possibilities, mostly negative, creating one more worst case scenario, allowing our ever imaginative thoughts to wander, recalling people we've known somewhere--that one where it so suddenly happened to her, or the other one where he went so fast, or the one where she fought so bravely for so long, and the one that so heavily weighs on you just now, the one you await--yours: "What will the one word be: Benign? Malignant?"

It's just one word; but what a difference one word can make.

Cancer kills more than 1,500 Americans a day and costs over $200 billion a year in medical bills and lost productivity. In Lori's case the particular biopsy was for breast cancer, a cancer which about 1 in 8 women will develop in the course of their lifetime. Almost 40,000 women were expected to die from breast cancer in 2010. Only one other cancer, lung cancer, claims the lives of more women in the U.S.

You are probably thinking of people's names as your read those statistics. Maybe they died this last year or perhaps they are battling cancer today. Maybe the name you are thinking of is your own because you are struggling with this disease.

And so Lori and I waited for that word: benign or malignant.

"The word 'benign' has to be the most beautiful word in the English language," one of my friends later declared.

"Then 'malignant' has to be the ugliest," a second quipped.

I know something of that. My first wife, Katri, died of breast cancer after a six year fight with that formidable foe. In her unfortunate case, the news came like a terrorist bomb on a peaceful parade, exploding on us as we hypothesized the cause for her mysterious symptoms, scratching our heads, all of us, including doctors--experts looking in the wrong direction, searching for the cause of her pain, examining relentlessly--until the disease, with a Jared Lee Loughner smirk, proudly exposed its sinister self, and snickering at our surprise, "ha!" went on to announce with warped glee, "Breast cancer it is, fourth stage, metastasized to the bones." And that was the cause for her pain, a pain among many that would dominate the remaining 6 years of her young life.

And now this day, Lori and I anxiously awaited her test results:

2:30 p.m., "I'm good, how 'bout you?" I tried to exude confidence.

3:00 p.m, "Half way there, they should call any time now." I was still attempting to console.

3:30 p.m., "It's okay, but what's taking them?" I tried to remain upbeat.

3:45 p.m.: "Maybe you should call and see if they forgot." Now I was getting aggravated.

3:55 p.m.: "For goodness sakes, what's wrong? Just call!" Frustration had found a parking place in my soul.

3:59 p.m.: Finally, the phone rings, Lori answers. My ears are attuned. Life hangs in the balance,
"Okay, Yes... Yes... Yes. Thank you. Oh, thank you for the good news!"

"Benign."

I sigh with relief.

Just one word. A wonderful word. Not malignant. Benign. Praise God!

"The Lord giveth."

"The Lord taketh away."

In just one word.

For now, I'll rejoice in the "giveth" and in that one word: "benign"--at that moment the most beautiful word I could have heard.

Until it's time for another test.

But that's another day.

This Valentine's Day: Send a Love Letter--February 7, 2011

> Gimme a ticket for an aeroplane,
> Ain't got time to take a fast train.
> Lonely days are gone, I'm a-goin' home,
> 'Cause my baby just a-wrote me a letter.
> --"The Letter," The Box Tops, 1967

My heart beat faster as I slowly opened the mail box. Was it there? Did she write? Three weeks of anticipation was wearing on me, three weeks of fumbling through the mail, three weeks of mumbling, "That's not it, not that one, nope, not that one either," three weeks of closing the mail box, sighing to myself and then hoping for tomorrow. I was about to break under the pressure.

And then it arrived: the letter.

And so began a flurry of love letters between Lori and me. Well, at first they couldn't be classified as love letters. We weren't "there" yet. But we would move in that direction. And soon I would write her weekly love letters. I even vowed to continue my practice of writing weekly love letters after we were married.

And I did for a while. But gradually, the weekly flow of love letters trickled into one a month and then dribbled into an occasional note. The Don Juan of love letters collapsed into the reticence of Briscoe Darling's boys.

It happens. There are kids to raise, bills to pay, laundry to wash, a house to clean, meals to cook--not to mention responsibilities of the day job. And in the midst of all that, Lori and I got connected to the internet, and we learned to text.

With life as busy as it is, it's so much easier and quicker to text a, "Love you," or email an, "I was just thinking of you when I read this article I've enclosed." It's not necessarily that romance has waned, it's simply more convenient to tweet your sweet, to communicate by email rather than by snail mail, to send an instant message rather that find paper and pen, and struggle with hand writing.

But yet, there is something about getting that handwritten letter and seeing love words written in that color of ink on that particular stationary. Lori still has a letter I wrote her from Bangalore, India over thirty years ago. I can read the writing just now (even then I didn't properly cross my t's), and she cherishes a card and letter I sent her when I was a lovesick freshman at Baylor University. How much nicer and neater I wrote back then. Was it because I took more time?

Time, that's it. It takes time to write love letters. Time--something we seem short on. The express lane of life moves too quickly to slow down for romance.

When I was home several months ago, I read love letters my dad wrote my mom when he was stationed with a medical unit in Korea during that war. Dad filled lonely nights--no television, no internet, no cell phones--with writing letters to Mom. Those love letters are now sixty something years old, but the faded ink still shines with passion and drips with the longing Dad had for Mom. I carefully handled the fragile, military issued stationary and imagined what kind of pen Dad used when he wrote those letters in some M*A*S*H* like tent on some cold winter's night, warmed as he must have been by the flame of love.

But it didn't end in Korea. I also read a more recent love letter of his. "I am so glad we met at the tennis courts some 66 years ago," Dad wrote. "You still look cute and beautiful to me. And you still have that quality of life that inspires and excites me!!!"

I read where, according to a survey, 2/3 of women ages 18-70, said their most cherished gift on Valentine's Day wouldn't be that diamond, that luxurious dinner at a five-star restaurant, that trip to an exotic resort, nor a dozen roses. It would be a letter, a letter!--a signed letter, handwritten by their lover, sealed and delivered by mail.

Did you get that?

So here's my challenge: Mark out some time, maybe thirty minutes to an hour between now and Valentine's, get a pen and some paper, go to a place where you can have the quiet to write, and simply tell your lover how much you love him or her. Be specific. Give examples of what your lover does that you admire, and what your lover is and means to you. Make it personal. Write from your heart. The main thing is to do it.

That's exactly what I am going to do this Valentine's. I'm going back to the good old fashioned handwritten love letter. Then I'm putting a stamp on it and mailing it.

But please don't tell Lori. I want to surprise her.

"Lord, I want to thank you for my smokin' hot wife.."—August 10, 2011

No, I didn't say it! (My wife warned me if I prayed that publicly it might be my last prayer.) Those are the words of the Reverend Joe Nelms, Pastor of the First Baptist Church of Lebanon, Tn., praying at NASCAR's Federated 300 Nationwide Series Race in Nashville, Saturday last week. Pastor Nelms became an instant star on the internet with comments about his prayer ranging from "the greatest prayer ever," to "blasphemous."

It is neither.

As far as I can tell, it's simply the heartfelt prayer of a man, in this case a pastor and life-long NASCAR fan (this wasn't the first time he has prayed at a NASCAR event), who didn't want to pray what he called, "the cookie-cutter prayer." Every NASCAR event begins with an invocation, and like most prayers before public events, they are generally quite the same. And most people don't pay attention.

But Pastor Nelms woke them. The Bible says we should give thanks in all things, and that's exactly what Nelms did. He thanked the Lord for Toyotas, Dodges, and Fords, for Sunoco racing fuel, for GM performance, and most of all, as he put it, "Lord, I want to thank you for my smokin' hot wife tonight, Lisa..."

Actually, Nelms adapted the line about his wife from Ricky Bobby's (Will Farrell) prayer to Baby Jesus in the movie, *Talladega Nights*. Pastor Nelms was, I believe, trying to communicate something spiritual in a humorous way.

Our church custodian picked up on it, although he may not have realized it at the time. On Monday morning of last week, as I arrived at church, he summarized the latest weekend news (he does this most Mondays), and at the top of his broadcast was the story of Reverend Nelms' prayer. My instinctive response was, "Well, is she? (Smokin' hot, that is.)

"I don't know," he said, "she must be to him."

Good answer.

With all the publicity about his prayer, pictures of the Reverend Nelms and his wife were all over the internet. If by "hot" one means a female that resembles Ricky Bobby's wife, Carley (Leslie Bibb), or Miss Sprint Cup (any Miss Sprint Cup), then Ms. Nelms isn't there. And some of the snide remarks posted on the internet made that observation. But they've missed the deeper lesson.

If she's "hot" to Pastor Nelms, that's all that matters. She, or anyone--male or female--doesn't have to fit the American cultural image of "hot" to be "hot."

Security in a long term relationship must have as its basis something more than mere physical attraction. In a recent poll taken by askmen.com and cosmopolitan.com, half of the men surveyed say they would drop their partner if she gained weight. Twenty percent of the women said the same. Maybe we've let the Miss Sprint Cup and Dallas Cowboy Cheerleader image of "hot" determine what's acceptable and what's not for us. But sooner or later we will be disappointed.

The important thing is to love and appreciate the one you are with, extending unconditional acceptance in relationships.

It works both ways--for male and female--this expression of gratitude for the one you are with. And there are benefits to being grateful; sometimes it ricochets back in unexpected ways.

When things get a little tense on my home front, as they invariably do in most normal relationships, when an annoying habit of mine (Did I just admit to having those?) grates on my wife's last nerve, when I see those beautiful eyes start to narrow (signaling anger), her right foot begin tapping (a sign of frustration), her pretty face turning away from me (a sure indication of exasperation, warning me of imminent danger), I know it's time for the NASCAR PRAYER.

I look heavenward, stretch my arms wide, and utter those words, "Lord, I want to thank you for my smokin' hot wife."

Her frown instantly transforms into that familiar cute grin as she coyly turns her face back towards me, rolls her eyes and exclaims, "Oh, you!"

Ahh, God has once again intervened. And lo! I am forgiven.

And then my prayer she doesn't hear, "Lord, I really do thank you for my smokin' hot wife...

And for your mercy!

Happy at home with your best friend--February 2012

"I'm happy at home
You're my best friend"
--Queen, "You're My Best Friend" (1975)

"How would you describe us, now that we're almost eight years into our marriage?"

Lori asked me that question after the evening news. For a second I thought we had accidentally clicked the remote from the news to a "Dating Game" rerun. I still have no clue what prompted her to ask that question, and she doesn't either, because I later asked her. It's the kind of question that could spark some interesting dynamics in a small group discussion on marriage.

It could even be rephrased as question for a couple contemplating marriage. "How would you describe yourself at this point in your relationship?" Or, as a question probing a couple's vision for their marriage, it might sound like this: "How do you hope you will describe yourselves after you've been married five, ten, fifteen years?"

But, the question was for me and not a hypothetical couple or discussion group.

The words came spontaneously from my mouth: "Best friends," I said, without hesitating.

Immediately I wondered how I let the words slip out of my mouth so quickly. Had I said the wrong thing? Normally I am one to pause and think before answering.

But from her smile, I knew I must have said the right thing.

It was the truth, anyway.

You see, my wife is not simply a friend, as if I have other friends with whom I share my life equally. No, she is my best friend--the one I go to with my most intimate thoughts: my deepest fears and highest hopes, my most profound joys and simplest pleasures, my greatest successes and most miserable failures.

Our marriage isn't perfect; we're both human. But it's fun; we're fulfilled; and we still look forward to sharing another day together.

Is it possible to be your mate's best friend if you're not already?

I think so. You can start by working on yourself before you work on your mate. When you stop trying to make your mate into the kind of best friend you want and start working on yourself to be that person, you are at least on the right track.

Second, pay attention. Not only does paying attention mean that you listen, and I mean really listen to your mate, but that you are also paying attention to what you are saying. Are your words often commanding and demanding? Are they frequently negative? Would you talk to a best friend the way you talk to your mate?

Third, analyze that. By "that," I mean arguments. Ask each other what words and comments trigger an argument. When do most of your arguments occur? Learn to procrastinate when arguing. "Look," you might say, "we're both tired. Let's get some rest and come back to this tomorrow." Often, after resting, or simply calming down, what seemed like an irreconcilable disagreement no longer seems worth discussing.

Fourth, give a compliment, then follow it with a hug. Say something positive about your mate in the morning and then again in the evening. That's a minimum. And each time, find a way to hug. Couples often feel unappreciated and disconnected. Complimenting and hugging can help each other's self esteem and bring each closer together.

Finally, remember you are most vulnerable to pride whenever you are most certain you are right. A proud, self-righteous person is not easy to live with. And most people like that have few if any real friends. If you want your spouse to be your best friend, forget about thinking you have to be right. Think of the time squandered arguing about who is right. Ask yourself, is this the best way to express my love and spend our lives?

My five suggestions are only that, suggestions. And they are not exhaustive. But they've worked for us when we've followed them. I wish I were better at it, but I'm improving, at least my wife says I am. And, when it comes to evaluating our relationship, she's the one whose opinion counts the most.

After all, she's my best friend.

When it comes to marriage, religion matters--July 11, 2012

It's wedding season; May through August are the most popular months for marriage ceremonies. While planning a wedding, depending on the elaborateness of the ceremony and number of guests attending, can involve months of preparation---thriving in a marriage is a lifelong project, filled with challenges. Somebody said in marriage there are three rings: engagement ring, wedding ring, and suffering.

One of the most important aspects of a successful marriage is often overlooked and that is the role religion plays in a marriage, or to be more accurate, the dynamic of spirituality in loving relationships.

The recent split between Katie Holmes and Tom Cruise, with his commitment to the Church of Scientology supposedly having a role in her decision to divorce, is a stark reminder that in marriage, religion does matter.

The reason religion matters is because we are not only physical and emotional beings but spiritual ones as well. When we disregard that aspect of ourselves, we neglect something real and vital to our wholeness and wellness. As the French Jesuit priest and philosopher Pierre Teilhard de Chardin put it, "We are not physical beings having a spiritual experience. We are spiritual beings having a physical experience."

Physical, emotional, and spiritual intimacy are all essential to a fulfilling relationship where two people become one while maintaining their unique identities.

In *Couples who Pray*, authors Squire Rushnell and Louis DuArt challenge couples to pray together aloud for five minutes a day for 40 days, promising that the deeper level of spiritual intimacy will lead to a more fulfilling sex life. The authors maintain that love making, romance, and conversation increase 20-30% when couples practice praying aloud together and fear of divorce diminishes to 0%.

I'm not interested in the quality of Holmes' and Cruise's intimate life. However, Cruise's commitment to his faith and Holmes' apparent lack of the same appears to have created a rift.

Holmes was raised a Roman Catholic. Whether her conversion to Scientology was sincere and deliberate or a cavalier decision made in the heat of romance may be argued by both parties. According to *Us Weekly*, Holmes is fed up with Scientology's rules and its demands of child rearing. The couple has one daughter, six-year old, Suri.

The venture of enjoying an intimate spiritual relationship within a marriage when the couple has totally different religious beliefs requires understanding, respect, and tolerance on the part of both people. The more convinced one partner is that his/her religious beliefs are the only legitimate expression of spirituality, the more problematic any unity becomes and the more likely the prospects are for a conflicted relationship. It's usually when children come into the picture that suppressed reservations of the other partner's beliefs emerge.

Tom Cruise is a devout member of Scientology, which maintains that our problems began 75 million years ago when Xenu, dictator of the "Galactic Confederacy," brought alien beings to our planet, placed them in volcanoes around the world, then vaporized them with hydrogen bombs, scattering the beings' spiritual essences across the atmosphere until they attached themselves to humans, harming us spiritually, resulting in a plague of psychological and social problems, maladies from which only Scientology can free us through a process called auditing.

When it comes to religion, you might say Tom is from Galactica; Katie is from Rome.

Mark Ebner, who has reported on celebrities and Scientology for 15 years, said on the Today Show, "When it comes to Hollywood couplings within Scientology, either you're in or out. There's no half measures there. If you're out, the marriage is as good as over."

To be sure, couples of different religions can have fulfilled, intimate marriages. And couples with identical religious beliefs can have failed ones.

But all things being equal, the closer a couple is spiritually, the easier it is to find intimacy at other levels as well, with each strengthening the next.

Until two unique individuals, one from Mars the other from Venus, find themselves gradually becoming as one on Earth.

Chapter Three

Parenting Matters

***Our Fantasy with Reality*--January 16, 2010**

> "Robin is better than the girl of my dreams. She's real."
> --From *(500) Days of Summer*

Our obsession with reality television has run amuck.

I sincerely hope Kate and Jon Gosselin get back together with their eight and live happily ever after, that Michaele and Tareq Salahi--the couple who managed to crash the White House dinner party--get their own reality show (maybe uninvited guests can show up?), that Richard and Mayumi Heene, who allegedly perpetrated the "balloon boy hoax" in hopes of landing their own reality show, learn from their mistakes and live a meaningful life, and that Chris Harrison finds the true love he is looking for among the 25 beautiful babes on the latest reality series, "The Bachelor," but I doubt if any of my 2010 wishes for these fame mongers will abate the onslaught of dozens of others who are ready to step up, and take their place in the media's spotlight.

You have to ask, just what are we saying about ourselves?

Could it be that we are simply trying to find significance in a world of constant degradation for all that seems wholesome and good, where silent acts of valor in the home are just that: actions that are known only to family, or perhaps only in the memory bank of a discouraged parent? Ours is a world where for too many, time invested in others doesn't seem to matter unless it's on DVD, where we can show and tell, and declare our lives--good or bad--for all to see, and for all to recognize--most of all... us. That's right, us!

But it's a fantasy world, after all, this world with its made up stars, this world we have allowed the media to create, and if we aren't careful, we will allow the lure of the media to enamor us and therefore ruin our silent actions of care and concern. The stark reality is that the majority of our good deeds will go forever unnoticed and unappreciated, I am sorry to say--at least by those this side of eternity.

But this hidden side of life does affect the other, does it not? It's that part of our of our lives where we encounter others apart from what anyone else may ever know, much less understand, where our unseen actions transform the present moment into forever.

It's the hands of a praying parent over the baby in a crib, a mom with a tear in her eye as she puts her child on the school bus the first day of school, a dad glancing back in the rear view mirror one more time as he leaves his son at the college dorm, a mom who silently waits and hopes for that wayward child to return home from who knows where, a dad who sleeps with one eye open until his daughter returns safely home from her date, the girlfriend who painstakingly prepares a scrapbook of memories only she will appreciate; it's in moments like these, when no one notices, when no one else cares, it's these moments, when we sit and wait, and hope and trust, and try and fail and yes, lose our composure, but most of all those moments when nobody knows but only us and the Eternal, these are the moments that make the difference for us and our families... forever.

And so, at 2:30 a.m., I tiptoe into my oldest son's room. He's 19, home from college, for goodness sake! And then I quietly, ever so quietly, open the door of my two daughters' room as they are sleeping. They are practically grown! What am I doing?

Just checking, And praying.

No camera. Just reality. It's better than a dream; it's life.

Avoiding the Graduation Blues--May 7, 2010

It can happen to you most anytime and anyplace; all that's required is a stuffy auditorium filled with graduates in caps and gowns, a principal or president or superintendent who directs the program with boring predictability, speaks in a monotone voice with a staccato cadence, and of course, a guest speaker, who is prone to talk long after most have stopped listening.

And then, quite suddenly in the midst of this, you are overcome by the graduation blues.

It's happened to me, in lesser or greater degrees, every time I graduated. I thought with my last and final degree I had certainly earned perpetual immunity to this strange and mysterious malady. But alas, it struck me again just last week when my oldest daughter graduated from Eastern Kentucky University. In what seemed like a nanosecond, the blues enveloped me, time traveling me back to every crowded auditorium where I had once sat just like those graduates did that day last week, transporting me back to Altus, Oklahoma, carrying me down to Waco, Texas, lifting me to Ft. Worth, thrusting me miles and miles from there to Princeton, New Jersey, and finally depositing me in Louisville, Kentucky. It was the same scenario in every graduation ceremony: the anticipation of the event, the slight nervousness just before my name is called, the excitement in holding the diploma, then the deflation as I step down and walk back to my place, and finally, the uneasiness, the angst, as I sit down.

What causes this? I thought about that as I watched each graduate walk across the stage last week. I felt for them, entering this uncertain economic climate, a climate with stiffer competition for fewer jobs, and even if they plan for graduate school instead of immediately entering the job market, there is the reality of no longer being at the top but orienting to a new program filled with unfamiliar faces and unknown ways. In each seat in that auditorium, there sat a person facing doubts and fears about themselves and the world around them. A chapter of life closes, washed over with memories of friends who will move on. Even though they can reconnect in many ways, it is never really the same.

Anxiety about an uncertain future disconnected from friends only submerges us further into the deep freeze of the graduation blues. The fear is that all the fun that is to be had is gone. As Jenny (Carey Mulligan) says to her headmistress in the 2009 movie, *An Education*: "If people die the moment they graduate, then surely it's the things they do beforehand that count."

But, as Jenny painfully learns, it's not. Graduation day is a milestone, but not the end, certainly not of an education, which should continue for a lifetime. Graduation may close one chapter, but it opens another, and another, and another. In fact, every day is in some way graduation day.

The graduation blues are not all bad; they do serve a purpose: by forcing us to slowdown for at least a moment, we can reflect on where we've been, where we are, and where we're headed. It's okay to shed a tear--or even two--as we, diploma in hand, glance back at the stage. Yet, we can be happy: we can, after all step forward; we do have control of our lives, at least most it; we can walk boldly and confidently into the future, knowing we can make a positive contribution. The cure for the graduation blues lies in embracing them and realizing that we are what we choose to be, that every tomorrow has its own opportunities, and we don't die the moment we graduate.

Next week my youngest daughter graduates from high school. As she walks away from the platform, I will look forward with her to a hopeful future that's promised to none but possible for all, a future filled with possibilities but not certainties, a future we can shape but not control. And as I do, I will be thankful for everything, including the graduation blues, even as I wave goodbye to them.

Juggling Little League, Family, and God--July 26, 2010

I had heard the complaint before in other places, at other times. "I struggle with wanting my child to participate in summer little league baseball and still have time for our family events, not to mention participation in church," the concerned mother told me over the phone. "It just seems like we can't do it all." In her particular situation, baseball games were being scheduled not only on Sundays, but on Sunday mornings--a definite conflict for Christians who want their family to worship together. As a parent, and as a pastor, I understood.

This is not an isolated, local problem. *The Wall Street Journal* printed an article on July 21, 2010, about the challenge parents face when involvement in organized team sports begins to overwhelm families, interfering with vacations, stealing visits from grandparents, aunts and uncles, consuming weekends, leaving no time for family leisure and outings. Although the story focused on elite youth sport teams that often requires a year-long commitment, the gist of the report was that parents are pushing back and sometimes withdrawing their kids from these programs so that the family can maintain a more balanced and healthy lifestyle.

Let's face it; few if any of the kids who play little league sports will ever make a career of it. Even of those that play competitive sports in high school, less that 1% ever makes it to the pros. For baseball it's 0.44%; for football, 0.08%. If becoming a pro is the dream, the odds are not in your favor.

But team sports do have a definite positive side: sports can teach young people how to cooperate with one another in attaining a common goal; they can teach basic life skills--like how to deal with conflict--and develop athletic abilities for further participation in competitive sports. Involvement in youth sports has been traced to improved self-esteem, lower obesity rates, and improved grades in school.

So, what to do about the time constraints youth sports--particularly summer sports--put on families? The problem is best dealt with before the season begins. When we give other people the permission to establish our priorities, they inevitably will. If we let the city's little league game coordinator determine our summer schedule, he/she will. And it will likely be at our expense. A clear sense of priorities is the only way I know of steering the family ship through the sea of summer frustrations.

If the goal for your child's involvement is to make him/her a more complete and integrated person, then let the coach or little league committee know your goals from the very beginning. If your priorities are God first, family second, and summer league baseball third, then why let a summer sports scheduler reverse the order of your life purposes?

After all, just how much is that first place trophy worth, anyway? Is it worth tearing up your family's summer schedule? Only the parent can determine that. But remember, your priorities do reflect your values.

As a parent who rarely missed one of my son's little league games, I have observed that the problem of over emphasizing competitiveness in youth sports is more frequently driven by parents who are trying to fulfill their own dreams as athletes through their children. Kids will generally take the sport about as seriously or lightheartedly as the parents and coaches do. I recall watching a coach shout at a 4th grader in a city league football practice: "What do you think this is?" he screamed, "Fun? This is football; it's not supposed to be fun."

"Really?" I thought. If it's not fun how do you expect a child to continue playing the game? I switched my son to a different team with a coach who had a sports philosophy more compatible with mine.

Parents have to remember they are ultimately in control of their children's activities.

Here's the bottom line: If the parents refuse to have games on Sundays, or Sunday mornings, it won't happen, unless coaches are willing to import players from another part of the country. And if they are able to do that, some city has too much money and somebody is thinking too hard about how to waste it. Remember this: Youth sports are meant to be fun. In the words of Benny Rodriguez, in the 1993 film, *The Sandlot*, "Man, this is baseball. You gotta stop thinking. Just have fun."

Letting them Fly--August 9, 2010

"I'm doing better this time," my wife Lori said as I answered the phone, "I'm not crying... at least not much."

She was leaving our youngest daughter's apartment. No, they hadn't had a mother daughter spat; nothing negative had prompted Lori's emotions. She was saying "bye" to Madison... for the second time. We had moved her to Lexington, KY., where she will soon start school. Lori informed me it was necessary for her to return the next day, "to help get Madi settled." That was true, but I knew more: Finally letting go is difficult for parents, especially when you are the mother and the child is the youngest daughter.

We have had all four of our children, in this blended family of ours, fly to different places: We felt a lump in our throats when Mary-Elizabeth flew to New York City; we longed for laughter after Dave moved to Danville, KY., and we carried a heavy heart when Harrison left for Campbellsville, KY. But when that last one leaves the nest, it makes all the children's absences seem even more permanent. Now, when we returned home, only Baylor and Max, our two miniature Schnauzers, awaited us.

The next day, as I walked through the house in the early morning hour, an eerie silence reverberated through the walls, echoing the children's giggles, booming their music, resounding with the clamor for help with homework, resonating with the cry for answers to life's ultimate questions, like "When will supper be ready, finally?" and "Why can't I stay out later?"

But I've noticed several positives to this empty nest situation: I have more room in my driveway, making it easier to buzz in and out of the garage; I can rattle around the upstairs of our two story house in the wee hours of the morning and wake no one; I have acquired, in the past four years-- three empty bedrooms, giving me a morning, afternoon, and evening study--whichever I so desire; instead of planning weekly meals, Lori can ask me at 6 p.m., "What do you want for supper?" and I can respond, "I dunno," and that's okay; I no longer walk through the house at curfew, making sure the kids are in, checking the locks on the doors, turning off lights; and I don't have to rush to get in the shower before the kids deplete the hot water supply.

The most rewarding and satisfying benefit of letting them go is the influence those young ones can have in the world. Children, after all, are meant to grow up, leave, and make a difference. As painful as it is to let them go, it's more hurtful to keep them home when it's time for them to fly to freedom. Granted, circumstances sometimes necessitate a longer stay with mom and dad, yet even within those situations, parents can release children to new expressions of freedoms and the gradual acceptance of more adult responsibilities. Even when the children do leave, whether it's sooner or later, until they are completely independent, they most often return--some more than others--if not for a home cooked meal, at least to do their laundry.

Yet, when it's time, it's time. Good-byes may not be forever, but they are steps along the road to maturity. And ultimately, a child leaving the security of home for a dream, risky though it may be, is better than one who stays for fear of failure.

As I glanced in my review mirror at Madi waving bye, I was reminded of that episode from Andy Griffith, "Opie, the Birdman," where Opie Taylor has accidentally killed a mother bird with his new slingshot. Opie then raises the baby birds to maturity. But then, when it's time to let them go, Opie has trouble. Andy Taylor convinces his son, "to let'em go; let'em be on their own; let'em be free like they was intended." And Opie does. Each bird flies to freedom. Then, Opie looks at the bird cage. To him it looks "awful empty."

And Andy, the wise, sage of comedy, agrees but then adds, "But don't the trees seem nice and full?"

Having raised them as best we can, we let them go. And instead of looking at the empty nest, we do well to look at the trees--the possibilities that lie ahead for them, the fullness they can bring to others' lives--and with a sigh of satisfaction, say with the good Sherriff of Mayberry, "My, but don't the trees seem nice and full?"

Yes, indeed.

Surprised by a daughter's prayer--January 23, 2012

"Why don't you go with me?" I had asked my daughter to accompany me to the Abby of Gethsemani. She was home with us for a few days during the Christmas holidays, visiting from New York City. Mary had been to Gethsemani with me before.

"Sure, I'd love to," was her ready response.

It had been a long December, and in the middle of it, I wasn't sure this year would be better than the last. Trying to hold life's inevitable tensions in balance--the pull of decisions that had to be made, the push of the consequences that would come from them, the internal wrestling match that thrashes across the mind, sometime after 2 a.m. --had worn me down till I cried for a time out.

What "might be," was obscured by the fogginess of "what is."

I knew it was time to head to Gethsemani Abby. In the solitude of the monastery I would pray, I would ponder, I would percolate: God's Spirit would infuse me with a supernatural oxygen rush that inevitably refreshes, rejuvenates, revitalizes.

But this time was different.

Or so it seemed.

The cacophony of this world overwhelmed the quietude of that world.

My escape to Gethsemani appeared futile; I had carried the baggage of my responsibilities into the lobby of this holy place. Gethsemani seemed too familiar that day, too close to the anxieties of the outside. The cares and concerns of the world had invaded the walls protecting the quiet and calm of Gethsemani.

And it was my doing.

Mary and I joined the monks from the gallery and prayed as they prayed, chanting their prayers with them, singing the Psalms at the None prayer time. I waited for relief from my strain but found only heaviness; I couldn't seem to shake the angst of the world, even in this place of tranquility and repose.

Walking around the back of the cathedral after prayers, Mary and I quietly chatted in subdued undertones. Staring at the naked trees across the valley, letting the December wind tickle our faces, we stood in silence, the whine of the wind whirling in our ears.

And then, quite to my surprise, my daughter prayed for me a prayer of comfort, peace, and renewal.

Somewhat humbled by a daughter's prayer, my mind swooshed back to May 30, 1990, so many years ago, but only "just yesterday," when Mary, age two and a half, prayed for me in her own way for the first time: "I love you, Daddy," she told me after bedtime prayers. I took that in itself as a child's form of prayer. And a few days later, after praying for her at night, she proclaimed from her bed, "I wanna follow Jesus, too." Then a few months later, in response to my question before bedtime prayers, "What should we thank God for?" she smiled and answered, "Let's thank him for Jesus."

Prayers continued through the passing years.

Straight to that day in the middle of a long December.

And so in the dead of December, waiting for Christmas to come and go and remind us of life in Christ Jesus, I should not have been surprised.

Sometimes God speaks to us through the holiness of monks, sometimes through the beauty of nature, sometimes through the revelation of his Word, and sometimes through the prayer of a child grown to adulthood.

Elijah the prophet stood before the windstorm, but God was not in the wind. Then Elijah withstood the earthquake, but God was not in the earthquake. Elijah endured the fire, but God was not in the fire. Then, there was a gentle whisper. And Elijah heard God's voice.

Having heard God's voice in the whispered prayer of my child, I was ready to leave. And having left my momentary spiritual retreat, I knew the world still waited with the same stresses and strains, trials and troubles.

But all was different from within, for I--having let the still, small Voice hold me in balance within the eternal present moment, even as it passes and yet remains forever--was ready to embrace the long December, and seize the eternal, today.

Drive-by Memories--March 28, 2012

The yellow street sign warned: "Stop ahead," so I tapped my brakes, bringing my car to a complete stop at the intersection. I glanced to my left before releasing the breaks and stepping on the accelerator.

Then it hit me.

No, it wasn't another vehicle. It was a series of scenes from the past, swirling around my car, streaming by me one by one and all at once, hurling me back in a time warp before swooshing past my car like a comet, leaving me craning my neck to grasp another glimpse as I idled by.

I was passing the house we lived in seven years ago. It wasn't like I hadn't been that way since we had moved. But for some reason today was different.

Caught up in a past moment, it's suddenly a time when it's just the kids and me living in the house. On the front porch I'm checking the mailbox, anxiously awaiting the mail, anticipating a letter from Lori, who was then living in Edmond, Oklahoma. I had gotten her address when I saw her in a restaurant while I was visiting back home. Stumbling through my "Hello, how are you?" I stalled, trying to think of a way to get her address without her thinking I was trying to get her address. "So, can I put you on our church's mailing list?" It was the best I could muster. It worked. I don't remember if I ever got around to the newsletter, but I did write her. And so, there I am on the front porch, one hand holding the front door open, the other hand searching in that mail box for her letter.

That's what I saw when I drove by.

Then, around the corner in the back yard, it's suddenly a few years earlier, and Dave is throwing the shot put, training for the thirteen year old regionals of the AAU Track Meet in West Virginia. Before it was over, the shot put had divotted holes over most of the yard so that a stranger might surmise that a herd of wooly mammoths had stomped through eons ago, or maybe some aliens from outer space had misfired their laser guns and splattered the yard.

That's what I saw when I drove by.

Then I fell further back it time, still in the back yard, only now Dave, Mary, my brother, Mark, his wife, Joy and all their kids--Tangie, Melanie, and Brian, are throwing the football around. Moments earlier Mark had randomly announced, "Hey, let's go throw some passes," just as he had done hundreds of times when we were growing up, in hopes that I would become a decent football player, only now he said it, not randomly as we had thought, but to lift the somberness that had settled around our house like a heavy fog because it's the afternoon of the day we buried my wife, Katri. We are running after the ball, laughing despite the pain of that day, and I'm hoping no one trips in one of the shot put holes and breaks a leg, sending us to the emergency room on the same day as the funeral.

That's what I saw when I drove by.

Glancing back, because I've almost driven to the next house now, Katri is trying to walk up the ramp that the loving men of our church had built for her, since she could no longer step up the back porch. With the walker in front of her, she clickity clacks it along as she struggles. And I'm watching. And then I can't.

That's what I saw when I drove by.

Then, we are in our cars, leaving that house for the last time. I see Lori, Dave, Mary, Harrison, and Madison, and of course the Schnauzers, Skittles and Casey. Harrison and Madi don't remember much about that house, since they were there only a few months, but Dave and Mary probably do, and as we drive away, Mary peers straight ahead, but Dave asks me to stop the car so he can run back in and take one more look at his old room before we drive away onto a new and very different avenue of life, a life that speeds by quicker than you can read the street signs as you enter the next new town.

Or drive by your old house.

And that's what I saw when I drove by.

With Diploma in hand: an open letter to my son upon graduating from college--May 31, 2012

Dear Dave:

We watched as you took your diploma in one hand and shook President Roush's hand with the other. That was a great moment for all of us, for it signified the closing of one chapter in your life and the opening of another.

Now that you have your diploma, remember that it has meaning beyond the listing of your name, the date you graduated, and the school, Centre College, which granted the degree you earned.

First, that diploma means you are to be a thinker. Just because you've earned a degree doesn't mean you automatically know how to think or that you will continue to do so. I've known plenty of people who have earned degrees from prestigious schools, and having walked across the stage with their diploma in hand, never read another book, entertained a new idea, or forced themselves to stretch one mental muscle. Having isolated themselves in a cocoon of indifference, they languished in mediocrity rather than thriving in the fresh air of open-mindedness and challenge.

While your liberal arts education has given you an excellent foundation to think for yourself, you must still work at it just as diligently as an Olympic athlete trains for the games. Thinking means listening carefully to others, evaluating what's being communicated, and asking yourself how their ideas might integrate truth into your life, or conversely, negatively impact you and the global village in which you find yourself.

Second, it means you are meant to be you and no one else. Take another look at that diploma. It only has one name on it: your own. Your education has taught you the value of being who you are. When you are not you, the world is cheated because you have unique abilities, talents, and gifts only you can give the world. You have a purpose that extends beyond yourself, but if you try to live someone else's values instead of the ones you yourself believe in, you compromise something vital within yourself, depriving yourself of the joy that comes in being the individual you are meant to be.

Third, it means you care about others enough to give a part of yourself to them. Education, at its best, doesn't take place in a solitary cell in an online conversation between a student and an impersonal, unknown grader.

Those times you spent with your buddies at the fraternity house or on the intramural field, the time you gave to others on the Student Government Council, or the moments you enjoyed interacting with friends at The Campus Center, were important. They can teach you how to cooperate, work for a common goal, and have fun in the process. So much of success in life is about getting along with others and making personal sacrifices that enable others to succeed. When you do that, you yourself are succeeding.

Fourth, as you look at that diploma, remember the people that handed it to you. I do mean President Roush, of course. But I also mean others as well, people like Dr. Wyatt, who ignited your love for historical research, Dr. Lucas, who directed you in your chosen field of study, Mrs. Nash, who in second grade instilled in you a love for reading, and Mrs. Followell, the high school teacher who first encouraged you to write, and Glen Richardson and Coach Robbins, whose demands on your physical discipline helped make you mentally tough. And be grateful for all those people standing in the shadows: secretaries, teacher's aides, administrators, custodians--people who helped in anonymous ways along your journey to the stage.

And lastly, pick up that diploma and take it with you. Take all that it represents--the learning that enlightens your mind, the friends that are now a part of you, the work that makes you strong--and tuck all that in your heart, letting those things expand your mental horizons as they light the path to your future. When you strive for that, even when you fail along the way and few if any recognize the sacrifices you've made, remember: You truly are a success.

And as you find your way, having walked away from the stage with diploma in hand, look back and give mom and dad a wink.

And don't be sad if you see a tear falling from my cheek; it will be caught by the smile on my face.

Chapter Four

Mom and Dad Matter

Treasures for Mom--May 6, 2007

While rearranging some things and throwing away some others, my wife Lori, saw an old family Bible. "What's this?" she asked. I explained that it's a family Bible of a couple of generations. She eagerly opened it and began thumbing through the old, worn pages. "What's this?" she asked again. It was an old card. I investigated.

The card touched my heart. It was a Mother's Day card from my brother Doug and me. The sight of my brother's little-boy handwriting pulled at my heartstrings. I thought of his short life and the suddenness of his untimely death. The other reason that card touched me was the date it was given. Mother's Day, 1961. That would have been the last Mother's Day card we gave Mom together.

The only other item in that Bible was a piece of worn-out school paper, now brown with age. It looked like it was straight out of the old Big Chief tablet. "Will you be my Valentine?" it asked. It was addressed to "Mom." Dated 1961 as well. Signed, Doug.

Some treasures a Mom just can't let go. Those items had been in that Bible for forty-five years. I'd had that Bible several years and didn't know they were in there. Some treasures are like that, aren't they? We tuck them away in a Bible, or a drawer, or hidden place. They're too painful to carry all the time and too precious to release. So we hold on. There is something in that hidden treasure that helps to heal or at least soothe.

And, it doesn't have to be a card, or piece of paper, or something material. It can be that memory of a baby's first step. Or first ride on a bicycle. Or first day at school. Maybe the child's baptism. Those memories are not in themselves painful. They are perhaps poignant only as we pull them up, recognizing that a child is no longer there with us in the way as before.

They are growing up too fast or already grown up and gone. And a Mom carries a certain amount of pain in those beautiful treasures. It's a healing pain. So we hold onto memories and the papers and cards and whatnots that evoke those memories as ways of dealing with the reality of change, as sudden and unannounced as that change can be.

Think about that this Mother's Day. The treasures she holds are sometimes hidden. But they are there nonetheless. And the best we can do is give the gifts of love and appreciation that lasts forever.

Unspoken Prayers Sometimes Speak the Loudest--May 24, 2010

Sometimes it's the silent prayers that speak the loudest.

For years my mother has prayed for me on Sunday mornings before I preach. Last Sunday, Lori and I had taken our oldest daughter, Mary-Elizabeth, to the airport to fly to New York City where she is interning with *Harper's Bazaar* for the summer. As Lori and I were driving back from Mary-Liz's 7 a.m. flight, we talked of how we were excited and somewhat apprehensive about her opportunity in New York. And then back home, on my way to church, I asked Mom to pray for Mary-Liz as she was at the moment in flight.

Mom started to pray for her granddaughter, and in mid-sentence stopped. Thinking it was a dropped call, I looked at my cell phone, then spoke, "Hello? Hello!" Nothing. Then I realized it wasn't a dropped call or a dead area but an unspoken prayer. Mom's voice, a tad weaker after 88 years of life, falters easier than it did in younger years. And I could sense she was tired that day. But something else was happening too.

Sometimes we simply can't say the words. The emotion inside can squelch the strongest of voices. The intercessor whose soul searches for words expressing the yearning of the heart--a heart sometimes burdened with the plight of others, sometimes exuberant with joy, sometimes pained with past failures, but nonetheless seeking a connection with God, a God who receives the inexplicable, the unutterable, the unspeakable with infinite understanding--on occasion can only gasp for words. And that was what happened as Mom prayed. Her prayer was silenced.

But it was heard, ever so clearly. As Origen, the early church father of the third century observed: "God pays less attention to the words we use in prayer than he does to what is in our heart and mind." The Searcher of hearts is attentive to those desiring him, those desperate ones, those delirious for him. And when we, prompted by the Spirit of love are moved by compassion, care, and concern for others, even as we search for the Finder of hearts, then the One dwelling in us speaks the unspoken for us. This knowledge gives the speechless believer hope. The hope is that prayer, even when inexpressible, is ultimately the declaration of a life seeking its purpose beyond the self. As the Cistercian monk of the Abby of Gethsemani, Thomas Merton, said, "The purpose of our life is to bring all our strivings and desires into the sanctuary of the inner self and place them all under the command of an inner and God-inspired consciousness. This is the work of grace."

When Mom couldn't speak, I spoke for her. I prayed what I thought she wanted to pray for Mary-Elizabeth. But words were not necessary. They had already been spoken. Sometimes it's the silent prayers that speak the loudest.

Weather Watchers Watching Over You--May 2, 2011

I used to wonder why my wife Lori and her family are such avid weather watchers. Whenever we are in a storm warning in Kentucky, my mother-in-law in Oklahoma usually knows about it before I do. Not long ago she called me on my cell phone: "Are you okay?"

I had no clue why she asked. I quickly glanced around my office for vandals, felt my pulse and answered, "I guess so. Why?"

She didn't call me a doofus, but neither could she hide her surprise at my ignorance, "Don't you know you are in a tornado warning?!" She was in the process of checking on my wife and kids. (No, I didn't ask her if I was the last one she dialed.)

Thank God for people who care enough to warn others.

That particular day, I was the only one left in the building. I could have been in real trouble had a tornado actually hit.

My wife, Lori, is like her mother. When a storm awakened us at 2:30 a.m., last week, I only wanted to put the pillow over my head and continue snoring, but Lori turned on the television, watched for the storm path, and proceeded to call any of our children living in the vicinity of the storm.

"Why is she like that?" I asked myself as I rubbed my eyes and gave up on sleeping.

Later the answer came to me when she asked me a question. "Where would we go in case of a tornado?" As I thought of an adequate response (I didn't have one), I remembered what it was like growing up in southwestern Oklahoma during tornado season. When the sirens went off, warning us of a tornado, we would hustle across the street to the Parkers' house. They had a storm shelter. The men would then gather at the top of the shelter's stairs and watch while the women and children would huddle below.

And our source of information in Altus, Ok. was radio station KWHW. Lori's dad, George Wilburn, was part-owner and manager of the station, and he was the guy we listened to. George was by the necessity of his job, a storm chaser.

He had a few close calls with storms and naturally encountered people in dangerous situations. One time he was reporting on the path of a tornado when he saw a pregnant lady lying in a ditch. She lived in a trailer house and was trying to escape the oncoming tornado. George rushed her to the local hospital. "I thought she might name the child after me, but she didn't," he teased.

Chasing storms as a hobby began in the 1950s. One of the pioneers in that field was a man named Roger Jensen. As far back as he could remember, Roger was fascinated with storms. Roger lived near Fargo, North Dakota. The rumbling of distant thunder, the crack of lightning announcing the approaching storm, the swirl of wind in his ears--all this Roger loved, and he became virtually addicted to the thrill of the storm. Roger said he was "born loving storms."

Some people, like Roger Jensen, are "born loving storms." But storm chasing can be dangerous. The 1996 film *Twister* and the television series, Storm Chasers, both depict the risks involved in chasing storms. At one point in Twister, Dusty (played by Philip Seymour Hoffman) spots a tornado and yells to his fellow storm chaser, Bill (actor Bill Paxton), "It's coming! It's headed right for us!"

And Bill screams back, "It's already here!"

Storms are like that. All at once, they are "here."

My father-in-law was not a storm chaser by choice. But he warned others. And when he could, he would rescue people in trouble. That quality was transferred to his family.

What I interpreted as a storm obsession was really a concern for people who could be in distress.

So, when that destructive tornado descended on Tuscaloosa, Alabama and unleashed its fury, I didn't hesitate. I picked up the phone, disregarding the time, and dialed the number of my close friends, Butch and Cindy Larkin in Livingston, Alabama, not far from Tuscaloosa.

"Are you okay?" I hesitatingly inquired.

"We're fine, David. We're fine," Cindy told me.

Then I waited while she paused.

"Thanks for caring," she said.

Moving Mom and Dad--June 13, 2010

As I walked away from the emergency room, I felt a heaviness for my friends who had just brought in their elderly father. They were rightly concerned about his health issues. But their dad wasn't. In fact, he was angry that his adult children had insisted on admitting him to the hospital.

There he rested on the gurney, pouting because he wasn't home. His lower lip was turned up, childlike, which enhanced the scowl on his face as he weakly waved me away.

It's not easy parenting parents.

What my friends' father was feeling is normal for the elderly in those situations. Agitated because they aren't home, fearing what lies ahead -- "Will I get to go home? Are they putting me away? Why are they doing this to me now?"--they often react in ways their adult children perceive as harsh and insensitive. And at the same time, the elderly parents frequently view their children as cold and uncaring.

Reversing parental roles isn't easy. Being a caregiver for parents can take more and more time which can put a strain on the caregiver's family. Often there are unexpected financial commitments, further stressing the caregiver's family. Then there is the emotional toll paid by caregivers: "I can't stand to see mom and dad go down like this. Am I doing the right thing? I feel guilty about not wanting to take care of them all the time."

It's a growing problem in our society. As Jane Gross notes in her recently published book, *A Bittersweet Season*, never before have there been so many Americans over the age of 85, and never before have there been so many Americans in late middle-age--that burgeoning baby boomer generation-- responsible for the health and well-being of their parents.

The dilemma I observed in my friends and their father, I now see on the horizon for my parents and me. This Father's Day, I will be helping my two older brothers as we move Mom and Dad to a life care facility. Instead of the home they've known and the town they lived in for the past 58 years, they will be in another location and a different home--an independent living unit. In time, they can transition to assisted living or skilled nursing.

Because I live farther away from my parents than my two older brothers, they've taken on most of the responsibility for moving them. My oldest brother has taken care of administrative details for their move; my other brother and his wife, living in the same town as my parents, have taken on the herculean task of helping Mom and Dad wade through a mountain of stuff in their house as they get ready for the move next week and an estate auction next month.

I will be there; it's my turn.

Mom and I talk most every day, and I hear the repeated refrain, "I wish you were here." Moving Mom and Dad will be emotional for them and me. No longer will they be in the town where I grew up. The landscape bounding our lives will never be the same. They will no longer be where they have always been.

But they will be where they are supposed to be.

On one of my daily early morning conversations with Dad--which always begins the same way, "Where are you and your buddies eating breakfast today?" and ends the same way, "Love ya Dad," I told him about proofing one of my son's research papers.

"He really didn't need me," I said. "It was fine just like it was. But I think it gives him a sense of security just to have me look at it. I guess he likes knowing I'm there."

Then Dad told me something his dad, my granddad, said years ago. Granddad was in his late 70s and his dad, my great-granddad, was almost 100. (He lived to 104.) "Son," Granddad said to my father, "no matter how old you are, and even when your dad can't get around much like mine and is unable to do anything for you, there's still some security in knowing your dad is still there."

That's something worth remembering this Father's Day.

Mom and Dad won't be where they were. But, they will be there, where they are supposed to be.

And there is some security in knowing that.

Grateful for the generations who brought us freedom--July 7, 2011

The black and white picture of the B-24 on the front of the time worn postcard caught my attention. I flipped it over to find my dad's barely legible handwriting, smeared as it was by an aged water stain. It was postmarked, December 12, 1944, from San Marcos Army Air Field, San Marcos, TX.

"Dear Folks," it began--"folks" being the word Dad used to address his parents--"boy am I tired! We had a night/day mission last night..." He was in training as a navigator for the Air Force during WWII.

Dad was only 20 then, younger than my two sons. I've seen his military pictures: full face, rosy cheeks, bright eyes, chest thrust back, proud to be wearing his USAF uniform, anxious to serve his country, more anxious to survive and put his arms around my mom.

I was not even a glint in his eye then.

And his "folks," my grandparents, were more than ten years younger than me the day I read that postcard just last week as I helped Mom and Dad move out of their home town of 58 years, the town they returned to after WWII and the Korean War, the place they chose to settle, raise a family, and fulfill their version of the American Dream.

Tom Brokaw appropriately coined the phrase, 'The Greatest Generation," to describe the men and women who came out of the Depression, won the great victories of WWII, and made the sacrifices to build their world--the fruits of which we enjoy today.

Not all the letters in Brokaw's book, *The Greatest Generation Speaks* (1999), are from people on the front lines. Some are from those who did not see action but were nonetheless willing to serve wherever they were asked.

Roger Newburger was one such man. He was with the Army Core of Engineers on Oahu and never made it to the front. "I would have tried to do whatever I was told to do, but I think the guys would have been safer without me." Years later, after seeing the film, *Saving Private Ryan*, Newburger went to his car and wept for 30 minutes, so affected was he "because of what the real warriors went through."

My dad was a Roger Newburger--willing to serve wherever he was asked but grateful he didn't have to face the enemy eye to eye. Thankfully, WWII came to a close before he was deployed, and he served as a dentist in a medical facility in Seoul, South Korea during the Korean War.

My neighbor and childhood friend, Kim Parrish, had a picture of his dad-- whom I respectfully addressed as Big Jim--in his WWII army uniform. Big Jim served in active combat. Stone-faced in that picture, he stared intently straight ahead, as if he knew danger was imminent. And it was. I admired him immensely and begged him to tell me war stories. He refused, and I was too young to understand why.

Even though Dad was not in combat, I was no less proud of him and appreciative of others like him who were willing to go to the front, even if they never had to.

So, this Independence Day I shall not only celebrate freedom but remember and reflect on the sacrifices of those who served wherever they were asked--those of the Greatest Generation as well as the others-- generations of people who have secured for me the freedom to enjoy a day of celebration.

And I shall be sad yet grateful for those who didn't make it home to embrace their spouse and hold their children and pursue their dreams.

As I walk with Dad down the hall of the retirement center which is his and Mom's new home, he grasps me tightly by the arm to steady himself. His is now a different kind of tired than the one he wrote about as the 20 year-old navigator in training.

And as we walk, we pass two elderly women chatting.

"You say you have a brother who is buried in the country?" the one shouts so her companion can hear the question.

"Yes, yes, I do," her friend responds with like volume. "He went to the war years ago... but he made it back."

I'm glad he did.

And for others like him.

Especially the one who holds my arm as I walk him to his room, so he can finally rest.

But my stuff is not junk! --July 7, 2011

"You'll find you've brought too much stuff."

The words were softly spoken--almost as if to himself--by a retired Pastor, a resident of my parents' retirement community. He seemed to know by observation and personal experience: We take too much stuff with us.

I take too much stuff with me most everywhere I go, even to the beach. "Let's see, towels, sun screen, sun glasses, iPod, watch (do I need my watch?), keys, cell phone (do I really need my cell phone?), Kindle (can I even get service for it?), beach shoes--oh my goodness, I can't carry all this stuff!"

Even when I flew to Oklahoma to help relocate my parents, I took tiny versions of larger stuff in my life: a miniature shaving kit, tooth paste and brush, hair brush, and compact case of contact lens solution. The fact is, I take too much stuff with me.

And that's our problem: we want to take our stuff with us, even when we retire. And I suppose, even to our grave.

I heard the refrain again and again from other retirement home residents as they watched me breaking down the boxes from my parents' move: "Downsizing is the hardest thing I've ever done." Not looking up, I nodded in agreement.

My parents' generation matured in a growth economy that tended to equate consumption with success and happiness. Growing up on the heels of a Depression era characterized by lack and want, the accumulation of stuff in times of prosperity equated with security. "Keep that stuff; don't throw good stuff away; you never know when hard times may hit, and you or someone else may need it again."

I have a friend whose grandmother built a large room and basement, almost the size of the original house. Why? So she could keep all her extra stuff in it. Then she moved and built a larger house that kept all her stuff. Now, her son has another house to keep her stuff, plus all of his stuff. What happens when they die? Call the auctioneer.

During breakfast at the retirement facility, I asked one dear couple what had been the hardest thing about moving. "Leaving our home--our home of so many years and departing with most all we had in it."

My heart ached for her as I listened, sitting next to Dad, who was on his first day away from his home of 58 years, experiencing the same pain that lady expressed.

And I wanted to kick myself for asking the question.

It can be a disheartening situation. Dr. David J. Ekerdt, who directs the gerontology center at the University of Kansas, has extensively researched the matter of senior adults having to downsize. Based on his interviews with social workers, geriatricians, retirement community administrators and family members, Dr. Ekerdt has concluded that the sheer volume of objects in a typical household--including the tremendous physical and mental stress involved in sorting out what's essential and the psychological effects of parting with what's not — can lead to what he calls a "paralysis that keeps seniors in place, even when the place isn't the best place." In other words, possessions become an obstacle that often keeps senior adults from better managing their health and well-being.

My brothers and I could no longer wait for Mom and Dad to direct us in what to keep and what Dr. Ekerdt calls "household disbandment," that is, disposing of possessions. The house had sold, the moving van would soon be in the driveway, and the retirement facility would not wait forever.

It was painful.

We ferreted through photograph albums, newspaper clippings, clothes and more clothes--and more stuff, behind every nook and cranny, more, more, more.

And finally, exhausted, we fell back. But we had it on the truck.

I arrived back home with a mission: get rid of my extra stuff. I plowed through the overloaded mail box in my office, throwing away old journals, magazine subscriptions, newspapers, and the junk mail that was cluttering my life. I sighed with relief at my little accomplishment.

And then I arrived home. "The packages came in today," Lori informed me. The packages included the boxes of stuff I couldn't bear to see thrown away from Mom and Dad's house. "It was a 'package deal,'" I quipped, that included the pictures of my first haircut, my brother Mark throwing me the football, my brother Lowell in his 1963 Altus High School letter jacket, and my brother Dougie and me playing together."

No, that's not junk. Junk belongs to someone else.

So, I'm keeping my stuff...

At least for now...

Or until our kids can go through it...

Someday...

Somehow...

And decide what stuff they want.

Empty Rooms Filled with Memories--July 25, 2011

"All that had been used to make it a dwelling place, by my folks on back, by Grover and me... all the memories of all the lives that had made it and held it together, all would come apart and be gone as if it never was."
--from "Sold," a short story by Wendell Berry

The rooms were empty by the time I arrived. Except for a few heaps of trash here and there, and some stuff no one wanted, it was finished, done. The auction for the contents of my parents' house was over. And there I stood with my sister-in-law, Joy, and my brother, Mark, who had witnessed the whole thing. Now they were exhausted, the auction (it was 107 degrees the day of the sale, forcing one of the auctioneers to the emergency room with heat exhaustion), had taken its toll on them, physically and emotionally. Moving slowly, almost painfully ambling from room to room, their eyes darting over every square foot of floor space, they searched as if still expecting to find something beautiful and worthy, something cherished that had been somehow overlooked.

But it was all gone. All that was left was empty rooms.

They looked at me with tears in their eyes like I had arrived at the ER a few moments too late and had just missed the passing of a loved one. Glancing out the back window where I used to chat with Mom on the porch swing about life, and dreams, and why mosquitoes like me so much, my eyes blurred as I choked out the words, "It looks so sad when it's so empty."

I then walked through each room alone, just the empty space and me. It was my way of bidding adieu to the home place. And in each room I took a mental picture. I could almost hear my imaginary camera clicking as I paused in each room. I stood in the informal dining area, and click, I captured a picture of our family gathered around the table laden with steak, baked potatoes, fried okra, and corn on the cob. We were singing "happy birthday" to one of us.

I glanced across the room and click, I was taking a Sunday afternoon snooze over there on the couch, the Sunday newspaper draped across my chest.

Then I was in the kitchen and click, there was Dad watching TV while Mom was brewing hot tea.

I walked through the den when click, I got a great shot of all of us at Christmas, exchanging gifts, laughing, and then, click, I got one last picture of my annual reading of the Christmas story. My brother is smiling as I read. He always did.

I tip-toed down the hallway and click, I caught a glimpse of Mom putting on make-up in her bathroom, then click again, and I was in my old room sleeping in my bed, back home for a visit.

In the dining room reserved for special occasions I clicked and saw us at Thanksgiving dinner, turkey and dressing piled high on our plates as we stand around the table, pausing to give thanks.

And so it was, I clicked my way through the house until I arrived back at the place I had left my brother and sister-in-law.

Tears again clouded my eyes, but not for empty rooms; I had just filled them with memories of what they always truly were: spaces where people gathered to be family. And I could carry the moments, the pictures, with me, tucked inside the canyons of my soul, waiting to be explored again for the first time--a new time.

"I think I may come back tomorrow for one more look," I said to my brother as we left.

But I knew I wouldn't, for there was no longer a need to return to the old place when I could always draw on the freshness of what it was and is in my heart.

Chapter Five

Death Matters

The terminal of death that leads to life--**April 12, 2006**

Sometimes we fail to realize how transitory life is and how permanent death is. If that statement causes you to flinch, don't think of yourself as unusual. We are so accustomed to life as we see it, we forget that there is a life we don't see. It's commonly called death. We fear it. But we need not, for it's the life we live after the life we see. We are in a very real sense in the land of the dying traveling to the land of the living.

I thought about that just the other day as I took my wife, Lori, to the airport. Her grandmother, Granny Betty, had died, and Lori was flying back to the funeral. I had decided, with some reservation, to stay home, watch after our four teenagers, and minister to our own church flock.

I had checked her baggage on the plane, and walked her to the gate. We said our teary good-byes, and I walked as far as I could to the security check-in. We still feel like newlyweds; we've been married now for a year and a half. And so, we lingered. We didn't want to part.

I carefully watched as she passed through security. I would lose her, and then catch a glimpse of her again and again.

Once through security, I waved again, and she waved back, passing her hand from her lips to me. It was her way of saying, "I love you." I returned with the same "words" of love. Then I stood on my tiptoes as she walked farther and farther toward the gate. She turned one more time, and I waved real big this time, making sure she saw my hand, and the love I held up for her to see.

Then, try as I may to keep my eye on her, she finally disappeared down that long corridor we call a terminal.

Life is terminal, isn't it? Have you ever known anyone to escape the reality of death? No, as a matter of fact, I haven't. And neither have you. Life ends.

But life begins again, too. It does. It really does.

You see, just as I watched my wife disappear from my sight as she walked down the terminal, she yet lived. She just passed from my purview. She was still alive. She did in fact "take flight." Literally, she did fly.

We are all in this life moving toward this place we call death.

But we who are in Jesus Christ have this wonderful assurance. We have life in him. That means we live because he lives.

Just as I watched my loved one, my wife, walk "out of sight," so in death we see our loved ones pass from our sight. Yet, because of Jesus Christ, they are simply passing through the terminal called "death." It's real. It's **not** real. It's only an illusion. They are still there. We just can't see them.

The truth is, we are only separated by this substance we call time. It descends on us in a shroud of darkness, blinding us from seeing those who have passed through its corridor. But time is relative. Eternity is ever-present and yet lasts forever. It's here, and we wait to experience it "out there." It holds us back yet pulls us forward.

One thing is certain. In Jesus Christ we will be reunited. "For God in all his fullness was pleased to live in Christ, and through him God reconciled everything to himself " (Colossians 1:19-20) Part of that reconciliation will be the reunion with our loved ones in Christ. "Mark my words," Jesus said when he ate his last meal with the disciples, "I will not drink wine again until the day I drink it new with you in my Father's Kingdom." (Matthew 26:29)

Here's what I planned to do: I would pick up my wife up at the airport, greet her as she emerged from the terminal, welcome her back, and then and take her out to eat. We would have a joyous reunion. We would celebrate.

And one day, Granny Betty, and the rest will come to greet us, or we will go there to greet them, and it will be a glad reunion, as we are reunited in that terminal called "life." Jesus did say it best when he said he would not drink from the fruit of the vine until he drank with them in the kingdom to come. And so it will be with us when we see them get off that plane. Or, will they see us getting off the plane?

All I know for sure it that Jesus will be there, and our return flight is secure in his hands.

You Say "Goodbye," God Says, "Hello"--September 20, 2010

Last week while waiting to pick up our oldest daughter at the airport, I noticed that the security area for departures was only several yards from the arrivals area.

I witnessed a young soldier's brave good-byes as he held back tears, giving his wife one last hug--and then one more--while she, teary eyed, finally let go even as she held hands with her sister or close female friend, slowly walking away, repeatedly looking back over her shoulder toward her husband, leaning with her every step on her companion.

Almost simultaneously, only several feet from them, I witnessed a middle-aged couple greeting with open arms what appeared to be their teenage granddaughter. They embraced as if they hadn't seen each other for a long time. All three were smiling broadly, interlocking arms as they walked away together. "Do you feel like getting a bite to eat?" I heard the grandmother ask the granddaughter, who coyly replied, "Sure." The three floated on wings of joy.

Although they are only a few yards apart, the departure and arrival areas are separated by two worlds: hello and goodbye. As I anxiously anticipated seeing my daughter, I thought, "Next week I'll be there on the departure side. My time of sadness will come." Then in an instant I saw my daughter smiling (I nicknamed her "Smiles," long ago) as she reached out to me for a welcome home hug.

Although I have no concrete evidence to prove it, I contend that the space between life and death--this side and the other side--is a closer distance than that separating the departure and arrival sites at Louisville's International Airport. And although we may not all be living dangerously, we are living on the edge, never knowing when our time of departure here will announce our arrival there.

Heaven may be closer than you or I think. While the New Testament Scriptures speak of heaven as a place, it is not limited to boundaries as we know them. For all we know, heaven could be in another realm of time and space, adjacent to us at this very moment, here where only this life separates us from that other place, that different dimension.

One passes through the departure area; another walks past the arrival gate. We say, "Goodbye," Someone else says, "Hello." Only a few steps and eternity separates the two worlds. A thin veneer of life appears to our time and space limited minds as a veritably indomitable wall, a barrier blocking us from a life we don't know and often fear.

Five days later it was my time. Instead of being the happy greeter to a welcome home party, I was saying "Goodbye" to the daughter I would not see again until... until who knows? As my wife and I hugged and then waved bye, we had a longing for security in our hearts. We were saying "Goodbye," but who would say "Hello?"

As I glanced back at the departure security check adjacent to the arrival area where people were leaving and arriving simultaneously, people oblivious to the others side's presence, I was reminded that the God who is at our departure and arrival is also most aware of where we are at every point and moment in between, even when we can't, and sometimes don't want, to see it. The One who is waiting for us on the Other Side to welcome us home assures us of our safe arrival. In the instant we say, "Goodbye," He is already there, saying, "Hello."

Starting our car to leave the airport, I found a familiar and comforting security in that. I had heard it before, "I am with you always, even unto the end of the age." We say "Goodbye," even as He is saying, "Hello."

That's true for here and for there. For now and for then. Forever and for always.

It's More Than Just a Game--October 4, 2010

The program stands upright, encased in plastic, holding a prominent place on a bookshelf in my office. "Kansas City Chiefs vs. Boston Patriots, Municipal Stadium, November 20, 1966, 50 cents (including tax)," is written in bold letters, displayed on the front of the program. Beneath that announcement, a black and white picture shows Chiefs' quarterback Len Dawson rolling out, behind the block of fullback Curtis McClinton.

It's the program for a game I never got to attend.

My Uncle Don, Don Krouse, lived next door to Jack Steadman at the time. I was eleven years old. Jack Steadman was for four decades chairman, president, and general manager of the Chiefs football organization. Knowing how I, as a young boy, practically idolized college and pro football players, Don, with the help of Stedman, made some things happen for me. For beginners, Don took me to watch the Chiefs practice. Then, I was allowed into the Chiefs locker room where Head Coach Hank Stram smiled at me, shook my hand, told me to grow a little, and come play for the Chiefs. And, to this day I have a football signed by members of the Chiefs team that played the Green Bay Packers in Super Bowl I. I cried when the Pack beat the Chiefs.

But I didn't give up on the Chiefs; I stayed with the sport because of something I learned from Uncle Don. It was a small thing, and he probably forgot about it, but I never did. It happened on one of our visits to Kansas City. Don had done it again; this time we were to sit with Lamar Hunt in the owner's suite. And after the game, Don told me, I might actually have the opportunity to meet some of the players.

Unfortunately for me, as soon as we arrived I got sick and missed the game.

But the lesson was learned after that game I didn't see. Uncle Don tapped on the door of my sick room. "How ya doin' kid?" he inquired in his raspy smoker's voice, now even more hoarse from yelling at the game. "Thought you might like this." It was a program from the game, with autographs of Len Dawson, Jerry Mays, Bobby Bell, Chris Buford, and Jim Tyrer. Forgotten now to most sports fans, they were my heroes then. And along with that autographed program, Don handed me a play by play synopsis of the game. I watched the replay of the game the next day and had fun "predicting" what would happen with each play. Uncle Don had helped a disappointed youngster feel better, and more significantly, in the process he taught me a valuable lesson.

Football is football most of the time. But on occasion it becomes something more than just a game. Whether or not you know what a first down is, you can understand human compassion, expressed most often in small ways, in little actions, like giving a dejected kid an autographed program, a play by play summary, and a tender smile. As important as it is to make every effort to win, the relationships formed as one person cares genuinely for another trump the won-loss record.

I thought about that just the other day as I hung up the phone, having received the news of my Uncle Don's death. Staring at that program in my office, I recalled that moment with him when I missed the game but learned a lesson.

And for the life of me, I couldn't remember who won the game.

Always a reason for hope, even with cancer--October 10, 2010

The words had inadvertently found their way on the printed page; they were obviously not meant for anyone to read. Only two words: "No hope." But they said so much.

Too much.

They were printed next to the name of a cancer patient for whom we prayed. I flinched when I read them. No one is beyond hope--not even those who appear to be victims in the last stages of cancer.

Cancer is indeed a powerful foe. It's taken down the tough (Lyle Alzado, Mickey Mantle, Walter Payton), the entertaining (Bette Davis, Milton Berle, Jack Benny), the rugged (Yul Brenner, U.S. Grant, John Wayne), and the brilliant (James Baldwin, Steve Jobs, Enrico Fermi), just to mention a few. There is no vaccination against cancer, and no society is cancer free. You have a relative, or a friend, or a neighbor with cancer.

Maybe you have cancer.

According to Dr. Siddhartha Mukherjee, author of The *Emperor of All Maladies: A Biography of Cancer,* because we are living longer, cancer has more time to strike us, making it a "new normal," in our lives. In advanced nations, cancer attacks two to three people during their lifetime. But we are making progress in the fight against cancer. Although the incidence of cancer is rising, cancer mortality is actually going down, says Dr. Mukherjee.

And so we hope.

Yet even as we hope in advances of medical technology and the benefits of healthier lifestyles, we know our time is limited. As cancer victim Steve Jobs said in his commencement address at Stanford University shortly after his cancer diagnosis in 2003: "No one wants to die. Even people who want to go to heaven don't want to die to get there. And yet death is the destination we all share. No one had escaped it."

I'm not sure what Jobs's concept of the afterlife was. A convert to Zen Buddhism, perhaps his hope was in an enlightened state of rebirth, or a dissolving into a blissful nothingness. Or maybe Zen provided the underpinnings for a more secular form of hope with no need of dogma or revelation, where this world is all there is and all we need. *Christianity Today* editor Andy Crouch's observation in *The Wall Street Journal* seems quite correct: "Mr. Jobs's Apple is a religion of hope in a hopeless world--hope that your mortal life can be elegant and meaningful, even if it will soon be discarded like a 2001 iPod." As Crouch notes, for many in this secular age, that's enough.

But for others it's not.

For the one whose future was mistakenly labeled, "no hope," it wasn't. He clings to hope--a hope that he, still in the prime of young adulthood, will by God's mercy overcome cancer and avoid death, at least for a while, at least until he can leave the hospital where he has been confined for more months than he cares to count, imprisoned in a bed where he hears of life on the outside, of days other people enjoy, days of sunshine and fun, of breathtaking sunrises and glowing sunsets, of weddings and parties with friends, days stolen from him by cancer's curse; days forever gone, dissolved by the slow drip of chemotherapy.

As I conclude my prayer, he signs the cross--a motion of his faith--and I join him, as we both hope in something more than a miracle cure, something that's beyond death, something grounded in the hope expressed by the apostle Paul, "For our light and momentary troubles are achieving for us an eternal glory that far outweighs them all" (II Corinthians 4:17).

In the hope of that eternal glory we can rest, finding within it reason to live in a world bounded on its four corners by death, breathing the oxygen of a hope that survives the misery of our happenstance because it's a hope in the One who takes us by the hand now and promises to carry us home then.

In that hope, we find reason enough to live for another day.

And rest in peace forever.

Forgotten Things Remembered--November 16, 2010

I hadn't seen or touched it in almost 49 years. It was a homemade schoolbook satchel before the days of book bags. It belonged to my older brother, Doug. He carried it home the last day of school, 1961. Having completed the first grade that day, he skipped home from Washington Elementary School, proud of his report card and happy to be officially a 2nd grader. And I, being one grade behind him, was as usual anxiously waiting for him to get home so we could play.

And that was the last day I touched that satchel or saw my brother. That's because that was the day my brother died.

Now, almost 49 years later I was back home, helping mom go through boxes and boxes of things long forgotten. And we had only scratched the surface.

That's when I found myself holding a white satchel with "Douglas" neatly written in big, red block letters across the top of the bag. Drawings of sports cars had been sewn on the front of the bag. It was a bit soiled--definitely a boy's bag, a tough survivor of the first school year.

The satchel was just as it was the day he dropped it in our room to go out and play with me. It even had his writing tablet and the "Crayola Crayons," still inside. And tucked to one side, his report card, signed by Mrs. L. D. Whitlock every six weeks, with the lonely exception of that last six weeks, the one left to be signed, left blank forever.

Mom had buried all this in that box, entombing it in a crypt of memories, leaving it there these many years until I--reverently holding it in my hands as if it were an urn containing sacred artifacts of a historical memory--flashed back to that day 49 years ago, to that emergency room where the two of us--brothers, playmates, friends--were being treated after a car accident, and where I heard him speak his last words to me, "Am I gonna die?"

And I didn't know what to tell him.

When asked the question, "How long does it take to get over a death?" grief therapist, Dr. Harold Ivan Smith, says, "As long as it takes." Sometimes, perhaps especially with the death of a child, it doesn't necessarily get better, it just gets different. In his book, *Grievers Ask,* Smith tells about Izzy, Dwight D. Eisenhower's three year old son, who died in 1921. Eisenhower, a WWII general and two-term president, said of his son's death, "It was the greatest disappointment and disaster in my life... the one I have never been able to forget completely."

Holding my brother's 1st grade school satchel in my hands, choking down a golf ball size lump in my throat, and seeing the tears in my mother's eyes, I would have to agree with Mr. Eisenhower. And folding up that book bag, not knowing exactly what I would do with it, I realized as I carried it home, that in its burial, it had become much more than just a bag: it was a satchel full of memories, a bag full of grief, a receptacle of sorrows, the opening of which released images long forgotten, surreal-like as they rose to life, floating before my eyes like moving scenes on an 8 mm family film, portraying a little boy laughing his way home from school, wrestling his little brother in playful fun, chasing his dachshund to the car, edging his way in front of his little brother into the front seat, crashing onto the hood of the car, lying lifelessly with his brother in shattered windshield glass, crying in his brother's arms on the way to the hospital, asking little brother that final, most ultimate question, and not receiving an answer.

Memories have a way of apprehending us when we least expect it. Pain is the price we pay for having loved, and grief is the residue of memories long forgotten but always remembered.

Heaven, for Real? --April 4, 2011

Stories about dying, going to heaven (or hell) and selling books about it has become a veritable cottage industry these days.

Two pastors, Don Piper and Steve Sjogren, both wrote about visions of heaven in their death or near-death experiences. Piper's *90 Minutes in Heaven*, (2004) was followed by Sjogren's, *The Day I Died* (2006).

The stories of two children and their encounters with heaven were published in 2010. *The Boy Who Came Back from Heaven, A Remarkable Account of Miracles, Angels, and Life Beyond This World*, recounts 6-year-old Alex Malarkey's journey into heaven while he was in a two-month coma. The story of Colton Burpo, who was almost four-years old at the time of his surgery when he had his visitation of heaven, is described in *Heaven is for Real, A Little Boy's Astounding Story of His Trip to Heaven and Back*.

In Colton Burpo's heaven no one wore glasses, no one was old, everyone appeared to be in their twenties, but everyone Reverend Don Piper encountered in heaven was the same age they had been the last time he saw them--"except that all the ravages of living on earth had vanished." The people Colton saw in heaven had angel-like wings, a detail unique to his vision. Alex Malarkey's heaven is a lot like earth, only it's perfect and has a hole that leads to hell. Sjogren didn't actually have a vision of heaven, although he heard the voice of God.

Colton's father is forthright is stating that Colton's experience of heaven happened while he was in surgery.

Malarkey's injuries were severe, but he was never pronounced dead.

Sjogren's heart stopped, but neither was he pronounced dead.

Piper's claim of death comes from the testimony of those who were at the scene of his car accident: "Someone examined me, found no pulse, and declared that I had been killed instantly." It would be 90 minutes before another EMT checked on Piper and again found no pulse.

Could a distracted EMT have missed something? Or was Piper actually dead?

We can't know for sure.

What should we make of these accounts?

Dr. Kevin Nelson, M.D., Professor of Neurology at the University of Kentucky maintains that near death experiences are in the brain. After the heart stops, brain activity continues for another 10-20 seconds and develops other wave forms. As the blood flow stops, memories become very discombobulated.

Furthermore, during cardiac arrest there is often a small amount of blood flow to the brain, allowing the brain to go in and out of consciousness, even though those around the person don't know it. Nelson concludes from his research that in near-death experiences, the brain blends REM (rapid eye movement) with non-REM sleep, and this gives near-death experiences many of their important qualities. Out of the body experiences are a part of this phenomenon and have even been clinically reproduced by disrupting the temporal parietal areas of the brain.

During near-death episodes, people are likely to draw on life memories that are most significant to them--hence the visions of heaven and encounters with people of personal significance. Nelson documents his findings in his just published book, *The God Impulse, Is Religion Hardwired into the Brain?*

His conclusions would help explain why people of different faiths and cultures frequently have varying visions of heaven during near-death experiences. Other studies report, for example, a Hindu entering heaven on the back of a cow and a Muslim identifying the bright light as Allah.

I have no doubt that something profoundly spiritual happened to the Burpo and Malarkey children, as well as the pastors, Piper and Sjogren. I also am convinced they have no deceptive motive; they are sincere and convinced that the events they describe truly happened.

And maybe they did.

And maybe they didn't.

That's why we must not anchor our belief in the reality of heaven on such accounts.

Now, if someone were to come back after being dead several days, and in doing so fulfill a myriad of ancient prophesies about the event, and if this person were to live on earth in a resurrected body for several weeks before ascending into this heaven--well, that would be something worth banking a belief in heaven on.

Hmm, wouldn't that be the story about Jesus, the One whose resurrection Christians just celebrated last Sunday?

Wherever he is, that's heaven. Whatever it's like, that's where I want to be.

When you can't find your soul--August 15, 2011

The words surprised me, especially since they came from Grandma.

"She says she can't find her soul, and she's ready for God to take her home," my mother-in-law told me on the phone, her voice cracking as she spoke through her tears, trying her best to quote Grandma. By "home" Grandma apparently meant heaven. That made sense. Grandma had not been feeling well for days, and after all, she is one month shy of being 102 years old.

But her words, "I can't find my soul," puzzled me. She didn't say she didn't know where she was going or that she was clueless about who would take her there. No, she was ready for God to take her home to heaven.

Where is the soul, anyway, and why couldn't Grandma find hers?

For skeptics like Michael Shermer the soul is located in the patterns of information coded in our DNA and neural memories. In his book, *The Soul of Science*, he states that "it appears that when we die our pattern is lost." The soul is the mind and dies when the brain ceases to function: "Either the soul survives death or it does not, and there is no scientific evidence that it does."

But British scientist Dr. Sam Parnia, in studying heart attack patients, says he is finding evidence that suggests consciousness may continue after the brain has stopped functioning and a patient is clinically dead. Parnia is even conducting research to isolate where in the brain such consciousness is located. Would that be where the soul is?

Although he is by no means a scientist, I wonder if philosophy professor and literary giant, William H. Gass, would agree with Shermer and the scientific skeptics. With his typical piercing intellect, Gass states in his wonderful book of essays, *Finding a Form*, "I am going to insist that what we sometimes call the soul is simply the immediate source of any speech--the larynx of the logos--a world without words would be a soulless one..."

Grandma may not have known where her soul was, but she knew she had one and that it lives forever; she may have been momentarily confused about its place--was it somewhere in her neural memories? between heaven and earth? deep within herself, in whatever gives rise to words, i.e. thought itself?--but she was certain God would take her soul home.

Maybe Grandma was going through something like what St. John of the Cross termed, *La noche oscura del alma*, "the dark night of the soul," a painful, lonely time of hardship and suffering when God often seems far away and praying is difficult. When I called to pray for Grandma, she didn't feel like praying, (unusual for her) but was grateful that I would pray nonetheless.

In the midst of pain and suffering it's easy to lose our place, forgetting our souls, interpreting the darkness of the night as the obliteration of light, the fogginess of the moment as the suspension of forever.

But God is there even when we have lost our footing and feel like we are hopelessly slipping into an endless quicksand of doubt. St. John in his gospel, quotes Jesus as saying that no one or anything can take the soul of a believer because God's children are safe and secure in his hands: "No one can snatch them away from me, for my Father has given them to me, and he is more powerful than anyone else" (John 10:28-29).

Grandma knew God was there, really, all along, even when she couldn't find her soul.

When my sister-in-law, Lisa, called her and asked about what Grandma had said, Lisa tried to help her. "Did you mean the nursery rhyme you've prayed before, 'Now I lay me down to sleep?'"

"Oh, yes, that's it, honey," Grandma said. And then she repeated the prayer with Lisa, "Now I lay me down to sleep, I pray the Lord my soul to keep. And if I die before I wake, I pray the Lord my soul to take."

If Grandma couldn't remember for the moment, at least she knew where she could find her soul: safe in the hands of God who will keep it and not take it until he is ready for her.

Be careful with those words, they could be your last-- September 12, 2011

I was standing at the street corner, waiting for the light to change when I saw him out of the corner of my eye. He was waving his left arm from his car window, urgently trying to get my attention. Then, pulling out of his parking space, he stopped in front of me, blocking me from crossing the street. Only after he lowered his electric window on the passenger side could I see who it was.

"I liked your sermon yesterday; I liked it a lot." Extending his arm full length towards me, he gave me a wave of approval and sped away before I could even say, "Thanks."

Less than 24 hours later, Bill Hagen had died of a heart attack. The words he spoke to me weren't his last, but they were the last ones I heard from him.

Bill wasn't a member of the church I pastor. He faithfully worshipped at The Holy Name of Mary Catholic Church, but he would watch our morning worship service on television. Bill would teasingly say he needed a double dose, one from the Catholic Church and then another from the Baptist. I was afraid to ask him which was the most difficult to swallow, but since he smiled when he told me, I guessed both were good for him.

It would have been easier for Bill to have kept driving that last day he saw me. But he took time to stop--even for just a couple of seconds--halt traffic, lower his window, and speak the words. It doesn't take long to bless another, as he did me, but it does take time. And I will forever remember the last thing I heard him say.

What we say tells others what we are. And the truth is, we never know what words we speak will be the last ones someone else hears from us. It could be anybody, not just our immediate family. I was far from one of the more significant people in Bill Hagen's life; our conversations were brief and casual. But he paused long enough to say something positive that day. And that made a forever difference.

Even when one knows death is imminent, words are sometimes unwittingly uttered, and in that unplanned moment, those words reveal the character of the speaker. It is said that Marie Antoinette's last words were, "*Pardonnez-moi, monsieur. Je ne l'ai pas fait exprès,*" which translated means, "Pardon me, sir. I did not do it on purpose." She had accidentally stepped on the foot of her executioner as he was taking her to the guillotine.

Tallulah Bankhead's last coherent words were, "Codeine... bourbon." That will usually do it for coherence.

"Please don't leave me," were the last words comedian Chris Farley spoke to a prostitute before collapsing and dying of an apparent drug overdose. Those hauntingly lonely words from that funny man remind me that comedy often covers sadness.

When I think of all the stupid and insensitive words I've spoken, I can only give thanks that I've been given another day to replace those words with others, words that reveal a better side, words that can make a positive difference for someone else--not just the well-adjusted, the peaceful, the joyful, but also the hurting, the lonely, and the desperate as well, for the right word spoken at the right time is never wasted on anyone, regardless of their station in life.

And the best way to make sure it's the right word is to remember the fragility of life, life which comes as a precious gift moment by moment, is lived only in the present, the now, and expressed with words that will sooner or later be our last--echoing in the lives of others for the eternity we share.

Chapter Six

The Holidays Matter

It didn't feel like Christmas, Or did it?--December 31, 2009

"It didn't feel like Christmas this year," my daughter Madison, plaintively said, as we stood shivering in the 19 degree temperature at 5:30 a.m., December 26, waiting in what seemed like an interminable line of impatient foot-tapping passengers outside the Will Rodgers International Airport in Oklahoma City, Oklahoma, hoping that we would make our early morning flight back home to Kentucky.

We all nodded in silent agreement with Madison; it had not felt like Christmas this year. We had hurriedly left our family in Altus, Oklahoma, our Christmas having been interrupted by a devastating blizzard, hammering the state, causing the Governor to issue a state of emergency as it left abandoned cars, broken power lines, and stranded motorists in its wake. And for us, it meant a truncated Christmas that was already shortchanged by a depressed economy that affects most families, even ministers' families!

I thought about that as I stood there with my family in the cold, approaching the airlines ticket counter. For some reason, the airline was short on help, the cause for the bloated line wherein we stood. Whatever the reason for the workers' absence, it didn't seem to matter to Mr. Juan Barrientez, the man who was working as fast as he could to make up for his company's short handedness. Working without gloves because he couldn't write as fast with them, he fearlessly processed tickets, and dealt with the hurriedness, the complaints, and the aggravation of the impatient customers. And as I watched him, Mr. Barrientez, stood firm, taking the customers' assaults, somehow managing to say repeatedly with the calmness and sincerity of a hostess in a first class restaurant on a casual Friday evening, "Sorry for the inconvenience; have a nice day."

Only one person, as far as I could detect, of the dozens who hurriedly placed their luggage for Mr. Barrientez to tag, bothered to tip the man.

So, as I handed him our seven bags, I noticed his name tag. "Juan Barrientez."

"Mr. Barrientez," I said so that those around could hear the proudness with which I pronounced his name, "Thanks for doing a good job." And with that I handed him a tip.

Now, the amount of that tip didn't matter to Mr. Barrientez. No noblesse oblige here. He took the money without counting it, smiled, paused, and said in a voice that spoke from a heart that knew the more common rejection of common humanity, "Thanks, and God bless you. Merry Christmas."

As I turned and walked toward the warmth of the terminal, still anxious about getting my family on that plane, I couldn't help but think of a Christmas so long ago. You know that Christmas? It was the one when Joseph and Mary didn't have time to enjoy the gifts celebrating the birth of their baby, Jesus. No time for the birthday dinner, or the warmth of the manger, or the reception of shepherds. It was time to travel, to get out of Bethlehem and to Egypt. With their lives at stake, they had no time to pack. Just leave.

And surely, in the midst of the mayhem, someone, if only an angel, helped with a donkey, or blankets, or directions. And now, we know not his or her name.

For all I know it was Juan Barrientez.

And, then, like now, it didn't feel much like Christmas, that first Christmas. No time to enjoy family. Or presents. Or dinner. It didn't feel like a real Christmas.

Or did it?

Didn't that feel like Christmas, after all?

Christmas Gifts--January 23, 2010

Christmas gifts come in a variety of packages; but the best ones come as surprises, off the cuff, bouncing off the wall, where did it come from kind of surprises.

My wife asked me the other day what special Christmas memories I had. No way, stressed as I was with getting ready for Christmas, could I think of any Christmas memories. But, Christmas gifts, like memories, most often come in unexpected ways.

Don Hughes has cancer. That's why I know him. I visited him for the first time over a year ago. Some people a pastor prays for and that's that. But then some linger for unexplainable reasons, in the connection of heart and mind.

Don and I had an immediate rapport with each other, as dissimilar as we are. He is from a rural community; I'm a city boy. As wise as he is, Don had to quit school after the sixth grade so he could help support his parents, his father having been disabled; my education extended twelve years beyond high school. Don is of the "Greatest Generation;" I'm a "Baby Boomer." He is a devoted Roman Catholic; I'm Southern Baptist, of sorts. His family arrived in Marion County, Kentucky, in the late eighteenth century, helping settle what became known as the "Catholic Holy Land." I'm an umpteenth generation Baptist from Oklahoma. Don and I--we are a contrast.

As different as we are, our faiths intersected at the point of human pain. In this case it was the recurrence of cancer. Genuine prayer, born out of desperation, knows not the boundaries defined by the human restrictions of religion.

In one of our conversations about prayer, I had mentioned to Don how I would like to have a prayer bench, since I frequently like to pray on my knees. At the time I didn't know he was something of a master craftsman, an artist of sorts. Woodworking came rather naturally to Don.

And then, Don's cancer came back, after a brief respite. "I'll be by to see you in a couple of days," he surmised, as he told me his bad news.

"I'm here," I responded.

When Don arrived, I walked into the office to greet him. By his side was a handsomely crafted cheery wood prayer bench. I was totally surprised, taken back. Just a Christmas surprise? No, it was more than that.

We sat and talked as I placed the prayer bench first in one place and then another. And then, we prayed for hope, and healing, and God's comfort.

Don, paused, and thought, started to speak, and then pondered some more. I thought I detected tears in his work worn eyes. I listened as he slowly choked out the words, "I haven't known you for long, but I count you as a true friend."

Time stopped. Christmas happened. The best Christmas gifts come as surprises.

"Had any special Christmas memories?"

I had just received mine.

Back to Work, Hope on Labor Day--September 1, 2010

Was it a cryptic message from Above? Did the New York City transit system leave it? Or was it an intriguing ad, perhaps an experimental one, coming from Madison Avenue?

My wife pointed to the words as we, visitors in the City, walked through the block long passageway, known as "the path," between the Times Square and Port Authority bus terminations in the New York City subway system.

My head was down, and I hadn't noticed. The words she pointed to were written on the beams attached to the ceiling, spaced about 50 feet apart, a distance forcing me to wait until I walked to the next beam to continue reading the poem. Here are the words:

> *Overslept,*
> *So tired.*
> *If late,*
> *Get fired.*
> *Why bother?*
> *Why the pain?*
> *Just go home*
> *Do it again.*

The words, written by Norman B. Colp, were inspired by the old Burma-Shave ads of the 1950s, which used the delayed response of a jingle as an advertising gimmick. The Metropolitan Transit Authority commissioned the work in 1997. It was supposed to be displayed for one year, but the words, there in plain black and white, blending with the dingy, drab. subway walls, have remained for us to ponder. The work, entitled, "The Commuter's Lament or A Close Shave," was intended to capture the experience of everyday working people.

We left the subway, climbing the steps to 42nd Street, but "The Commuter's Lament" stayed with me. At first the words had struck me as satirical, the creation of a dry wit. But the more I puzzled over them, the more haunting they became. How many thousands read those words day after burdensome day? Did they prompt a smile? A sigh? Both?

The daily grind's relentless routine wears us down, ever so gradually but oh, so certainly, staggering our once certain steps, dropping us finally to our knees and ultimately to our grave. The awful awareness of life's meaninglessness, the human condition's hopelessness, descends on us--not all at once, of course, but in subtly darkening shades of gray--embracing us like midnight fog, until suddenly it seems, in an instant, it strikes fear in the bravest of souls and confusion in the clearest of minds.

We all want our life, our work, to count for something, to have meaning and purpose beyond ourselves. If work is nothing more than the monotonous repetition of the same yesterday and the jaded rehearsal of the same tomorrow, we are *les miserables*.

Work consumes a considerable portion of our lives. The person who works 8 hours a day, five days a week, beginning at age 18 and retiring at 65 will spend 97,464 hours working. If we are going to spend that much time doing something in the course of a lifetime, we may as well have a purpose in that something.

It's the white space before that last, final, line of "The Commuter's Lament" that pierce our raison d' etre. We all--well, most of us--have overslept; we all get tired of work; we all have feared for our jobs; we all have felt the pain of work; and we've all gone home. It's the repeat, going back to work again and again and again ad nauseam that's the rub. "Do it again," the poem concludes. But, why, after all, should we?

Working is living, and can and should be more than simply making a living, that is, unless we are content to be mere automatons, accepting the order of the day as the way things are and inviting discontent, depression, and dysfunction into our lives. The motivation to keep going is bound up in hope, which consists to a large degree in finding a higher purpose in our work.

So, on Labor Day weekend, 2010, when unemployment is creeping closer and closer to 10%, the work force appears less and less optimistic, and economic anxiety climbs higher and higher, perhaps we do well to take a note from a sometime unemployed but never idle tent maker of another century, Paul, the Apostle, who lived in a world every bit as bleak as the subway walls beneath 42nd street, a world where masters were masters and slaves were slaves, where upward mobility was yet centuries away. He wrote, "Work willingly at whatever you do, as though you were working for the Lord rather than for people." He lived and died for that. And never, to our knowledge, regretted it.

Not even for a moment.

It's in the white space before that last line that we find the reason. A worker's lament? Everyone's hope.

It's not too late for Thanksgiving--November 24, 2010

Have you noticed how easily we pass from Halloween to Christmas, from October to December, from "Trick or Treat," to "Here Comes Santa Claus"?

Did you bypass Thanksgiving yesterday? Apparently you are not alone. Only now it happens with greater celerity and casualness. We're beyond feeling any guilt about it.

I understand. I feel it, too. Thanksgiving's absence matches the seasons: October is filled with fall foliage, arresting in its brilliant colors of orange, yellow, amber, and red as the maple, ash, oak, and hickory trees reach the peak of their autumn display; December, with the Christmas decorations of green wreaths, red and white candy canes, shiny silver tinsel over boughs, is a month of anticipation: the possibility, the hope, for a blanket of white snow on Christmas Eve, the jolly St. Nick Christmas stockings in red, white, and green, hanging over the warm glow of the fire place, awaiting the descent of Santa down the chimney in his contrasting uniform of red and white with black boots and belt.

But Thanksgiving falls in November, when the fall leaves have disappeared and have to be raked, the tree limbs are starkly naked, the sun sets before you get home from work, and a gray drabness seems to permeate the universe with a dismal somberness. Thanksgiving, set in between the ghosts and goblins of Halloween and the Santa and elves of Christmas, doesn't stand a chance with its hapless turkey marked down on special at the local grocery store. Thanksgiving is in-between, and like the insecure middle child, seems uncomfortably out of place, having to fight for attention and recognition.

But it goes deeper than merely the differences in seasons. We Americans identify ourselves, the United States, as a consumer nation, and we do so with good reason: With only 5% of the world's population we consume 25% of the world's energy resources. We accumulate stuff and rent spaces to store the stuff we've bought on credit. And our lifestyle has come to roost on Wall Street with a financial debacle, in our environment with compromised resources, and in our health with overstressed bodies. We take and take, and stretch and stretch, for more and more, until we have made ourselves sick with Halloween candy and driven ourselves in debt with Christmas gifts.

We just raced by thanksgiving again, leaving it behind us, there with its lonely turkey in the middle of the table. We barely have time anymore to pause, and sit, and share stories with family about life, and memories, and journeys, so busy we are with our rushing, and work, and previous commitments.

We would do well, this day after Thanksgiving, to reflect on our thanksgiving roots, remembering that the first Thanksgiving was born out of adversity: A few pilgrims and Native Americans, having survived the harsh winter of 1620, gathered to give thanks for the harvest of 1621. Grateful for the basics of life--God, family, and friends--they shared some food, laughed, talked, and rejoiced amidst their grim circumstances. It wasn't until 1863 that the thanksgiving tradition became an official holiday. President Abraham Lincoln, spurred by journalist Sara Josepha Hale, declared the last Thursday of November a national day of Thanksgiving. You'll recall Lincoln's situation was less than ideal: The future of a United States was in serious question, the carnage of thousands of young men at Fredericksburg, Antietam, and Gettysburg was fresh on his mind as he called for all Americans to pause and give thanks for, "the gracious gifts of the Most High God, who, while dealing with us in anger for our sins, hath nevertheless remembered mercy."

It's still not too late to claim Thanksgiving, even today, Black Friday; we have time, if only we will, to draw on the spirit of thanksgiving past, pulling up a place and a time where not so long ago, amidst trying circumstances, people propped their chairs back, talked and listened to one another, reflected on life, and thanked God for it.

Doubting Christmas? --December 13, 2010

"Who gave you permission to tell Charlie there was no Santa Claus? I think if we're going to destroy our son's delusions, I should be a part of it."
--Scott Calvin, (played by actor Tim Allen in the movie, *The Santa Claus*, 1994).

"Some of the kids at school say Santa's not real, but I don't believe them. Santa is real. I just know it." My sister-in-law, Lisa Suriano, was quoting her 8 year old son, Cooper. "What do you think I should do?" Lisa asked me. "Should I tell him?"

I didn't need to ask, "Tell him what?" I knew exactly what she meant: the truth about Santa Claus.

Should parents tell their kids that Santa Claus is not real? Or is it okay to "play along," and enjoy a child's season of magical thinking with Santa at Christmas?

For some parents this is a big issue, and they are quite intense in their conviction: Participating in the Santa tradition is tantamount to deceiving children, setting up a situation that can cause a child to doubt the trustworthiness of the parent.

But for others, it's a healthy way of experiencing the joy and anticipation of receiving gifts. And, in those homes where the Santa tradition is welcomed, he is enjoyed for a while until the kids discover he is a myth. For some, as with our daughter Mary-Elizabeth and son Harrison, it comes when they see mom and dad, or an uncle or aunt, putting out the Santa gifts; for others, as with our son, Dave, it's another sibling who breaks the news about Santa's demise; and then for some, like our daughter, Madi, it's schoolmates who are the informants about Santa's fictional identity.

I don't think any of these children, although they may have been disappointed at the time, experienced emotional trauma at the discovery that Santa doesn't exist. Nor did it lead them to doubt their parents on larger life issues.

But, still, I have a concern here about how this plays out: A distinction should be made somewhere in the conversation with children between what is true about religion and morality and what is simply playful make-believe. I fear we may undermine the reality of the religious event we celebrate. We may inadvertently communicate to our children that it's all just a story, nothing more than a myth: the birth of Jesus and Santa; Christ's resurrection and the Easter Bunny--both melt into the same fictional genre: simply children's fairy tale stories we outgrow.

But Santa Claus does have a history, although it's embedded in tradition. His story grew from St. Nicholas, who was a bishop in a region of what is now Turkey. According to tradition, he was known for his love for his church and for the plight of poor children. St. Nicholas was reputed to have secretly delivered three bags of gold down a chimney to a poor family to provide a dowry for three unmarried sisters. From this developed the tradition of Santa Claus, a Dutch version of St. Nicholas.

Perhaps, by telling about St. Nicholas and how the story of Santa came from him, those who want to keep the Santa tradition can uphold the spiritual aspect of this season and still let Santa come down the chimney. Maybe they could say to their children something like, "Santa Claus is a wonderful story about a person who gave gifts and loved and cared for people. The main thing we need to remember is that Santa reminds us that God is the greatest gift-giver of all, and that's what Christmas is really all about."

What parents do with Santa is a personal matter; each family must come to terms with their own family traditions. But no matter what we do with Santa, it is unlikely we will shield our children from the possibility of doubt--and that includes the "real" Christmas. After all, Jesus' own cousin, John the Baptist, had his doubts. In prison, he found himself knee deep in confusion. "Is it true? Is it him? Is he just another self-proclaimed messiah? Should we wait for another? Is it just another story?"

So John asked. And Jesus answered, "Go back to John and tell him what you have heard and seen— the blind see, the lame walk, the lepers are cured, the deaf hear, the dead are raised to life, and the Good News is being preached to the poor. And tell him, 'God blesses those who do not turn away because of me.'"

Notice, if you will, Jesus never said, "I'm the Messiah, for certain; without a doubt, I'm the one." He only pointed to the evidence. He answered, but his answer still left room for the necessity of faith. For without faith, Christmas wouldn't be Christmas, would it?

No doubt.

Keep the Christmas Lights Burning--December 10, 2010

Now that Christmas has come and gone, what's left but to take down all those decorations? It's a task most of us dread. I suppose that's why some people leave them up until spring. And a few never take them down.

In my family, we ("we" being my dad, myself and brothers) would have them down by January 1, in accordance with the Book of the Law of my mom, who decorated the interior of our home. Many people contend it's appropriate to keep them up until January 6, Epiphany. Leaving them up beyond that date becomes borderline tacky, some say.

In any case, taking down decorations makes me wonder why I put them up anyway. Why do that? We did it, I suppose, because it had become a family tradition. Dad would get them out shortly after Thanksgiving, and I, being the youngest and smallest, would be ordered to shimmy up there or crawl over here to hang them. But my talents were limited; I was and am something of a mechanical incompetent.

You'd think, as much time as I spent helping dad put up Christmas lights, I would be a stickler for carrying on that tradition with my own household. I did for years but somewhere wandered away, and far from home, with my own brood up and gone, conveniently forgot this family ritual. Perhaps it's because I am such a mechanical disaster; beyond the simple task of changing a light bulb, when it comes to anything electrical, I can be dangerous. When putting up the lights, I would usually have visions of Chevy Chase in National Lampoon's *Christmas Vacation*, where he can't get his 25,000 lights turned on and when he does, momentarily compromises the city's electrical power.

Or maybe the reason I dropped the tradition was that I was indelibly scarred by memories of taking those decorations down, boxing them up, and carrying them to the attic year after year. I love Christmas traditions: the decorated tree, the mistletoe, even chestnuts roasting over an open fire--but I've managed to avoid the aisle in the store where Christmas lights can be found.

That's why I was so surprised when I found my son, Dave, home on his first day of Christmas break from Centre College, rummaging through the garage on Sunday afternoon a couple of weeks ago. "What are you doing?" I queried.

"Just getting out the nativity scene." He was referring to the outdoor nativity scene we used to put in the front lawn. I felt a bit shabby for letting Mary, Joseph, the baby Jesus, the camels, sheep, shepherds, and wise men lie neglected in the corner of the garage during Christmas. "And while I'm at it, I think I'll get that wreath down too," he continued. I felt a slight twinge of guilt; Lori, who was out of town, had mentioned the wreath to me, but her hint had fallen on my dull ears.

"Need any help?" I hesitatingly asked Dave.

"No," he responded "I can get it, but I'll holler at you if I do."

He didn't.

What's an outdoor nativity scene without lights? A trip to the store for floodlights and a timer for them, wire to hang the wreath, and a few hours later Dave had our nativity scene looking alive. And my lone contribution was holding the ladder.

Whether Dave knew I was overwhelmed with work in my study, or whether he simply wanted to protect himself from a dad's mechanical ineptitude, I don't know and won't ask. I do know he made Lori smile. "I love the lights!" she excitedly exclaimed the next day when she returned.

"That's Dave's gift to you," I informed her.

Later that night, I reminded Dave how much Lori liked the lights. "But let me ask you," I inquired, "why did you do that? Why did you go through all the trouble of putting up the nativity, the lights, the wreath?"

He paused a moment, smiled, and said, "Just carrying on an old family tradition, Dad, just carrying on an old family tradition."

Twas' the Night before Thanksgiving--November 20, 2010

I'll take the night before Thanksgiving over Christmas Eve any year. Christmas Eve is a tired ol' day, worn out by the flurry of activity preceding it, and by the time it arrives, usually too soon, it's all out of breath as it plops its burden of stress and strain--last minute shopping, checklists, nagging questions (Did I get her the right gift? Will it fit him? Should I have just given the kids money and been done with it?) --at your doorstep.

But the night before Thanksgiving is different. At least it is for me. It's tucked in between Halloween and Christmas, and if you're not careful, you'll miss it. While the world rushes to Christmas, Thanksgiving just sits there, calmly inviting whosoever will to come and visit a while.

Some families get together the night before Thanksgiving, and that in itself is something of a miracle. When they do, the focus is usually more on each other than in exchanging gifts.

My family would usually travel to my mom's side of the family for Thanksgiving. Grandmother's house was small, simple and plain. By the time we arrived from a three hour trip, it was well nigh impossible to corral my three brothers and me. But somehow they did, and we even liked it. In that little house almost on the prairie in Glencoe, Oklahoma, we visited with each other.

And I got to know my grandmother that way.

Soon we would pile in the car, Grandmother with us, and drive to Aunt Dee's and Uncle Leo's house where we would stay the night. Maybe it was because I had just been to Grandmother's, but their home seemed enormous to me. It allowed plenty of room for roaming, and its hidden nooks, which seemed to me expressly made for hiding, invited us boys into them only so we could leap out of them, scaring unsuspecting victims. At some point in all the jumping and running and hollering and hiding, Uncle Leo's booming base voice would bellow, "Time for dinner," and like hungry bear cubs running to their den, we would dash to the table.

And then the calm, allowing space for conversation.

And I got to know my aunt and uncle and cousins that way.

I hope we haven't forgotten the night before Thanksgiving because it just might be the best preparation for Thanksgiving Day. If we forget it, it's because we've lost our sense of thankfulness; it's because we've become consumers and receivers--getting, receiving, leaving, exiting: "See ya next year," we wave, rushing, with thoughts of specials on "Black Friday," toward another commercial Christmas.

Giving thanks isn't the norm. In the story of the 10 lepers Jesus healed, only one returned to thank him. "Where are the other nine?" (Luke 17:17), Jesus asked the one who returned. Like so many today, having received what they wanted, they were too busy to say, "Thanks."

Before you bypass the night before Thanksgiving, try pausing and enjoying it, even if just for a little while. That's what I plan to do. Hopefully, it will set me on the path to being more thankful.

So, I'm going to step outside, stare into the night sky, and if the stars are out, I'm going to smile as they twinkle back at me. Then I'm going to step inside and give thanks for my family, each one of them.

Then I'm going to call some family members who live far away and thank them for being who they are.

And as I drift off to sleep the night before Thanksgiving, I'm going to give thanks for a God who cares.

And waking to Thanksgiving Day, I'm going to give thanks for the smell of hot coffee brewing, for the glowing sunrise that chases away the early morning fog, for the blue sky or gentle pitter patter of rain, for the turkey and dressing with all the trimmings, for the quiet glow of the setting sun, for the twitter of birds preparing for rest, and for the cycle of life--even for all its spins, and turns, and starts, and stops.

And then, the night before Thanksgiving and Thanksgiving Day will be history once again.

But if we live it right, "thanks living" can become a way of life, making each moment a gift in the most wonderful time of any year.

Autumn Garden: Christmas Light--November 28, 2011

"You'd better get what's left of your garden in; we're going to have a hard freeze tonight," Glen, my gardening mentor, warned me several weeks ago. And so I carried in the tomato vines, picked the peppers, and salvaged what okra was left. In the garage, they are now ripening so fast that some are beginning to rot before we can get them eaten. My wife tolerates my boastful proclamation: "It's November, and we still enjoy the garden," as if this justifies the time devoted to working the ground this past summer.

Having saved what was left to be saved, I tramped through my garden late this evening. Only vestiges of life remain of what once was: Now, the garden lies fallow as winter approaches; now, it is stripped of life; now it fades into a deep sleep.

The outlines of the garden beds themselves preserve the memory of the high summer's sun that produced an abundance of lettuce, tomatoes, peppers, onions, okra, potatoes, and corn; and over there, on that side of the garden, I crawled from row to row, weeding, harvesting, sometimes lost in wonder and awe in that maze of produce.

And now as I slowly pace each erased row, I commit the remnants to their winter's grave: The plant labels--"Cayenne pepper," "Bell Pepper," "Okra," "Better Boy Tomato," "Celebrity Tomato,"--stand like miniature tombstones marking the places where the vegetables once grew. I accidentally step on a tomato or pepper resting on the ground, exposed, unburied, ghostly white--their corpse-like remains reminding me of life's inevitable cycle. And I feel somehow like I've intruded on their hallowed ground.

And the dead vines look like slender fingers reaching up from the underworld, desperately trying to grasp one last ray of life before they are mulched into the humus from which they emerged.

Yet, something magical is happening beneath the earth's surface as nutrients, helped along by earthworms, are preparing the soil for next year's crop of plants.

Christians have for centuries observed this interim time of the yearly solstice as an opportunity to anticipate the not yet--the birth of Jesus the Christ--even as they grieve the present: the dominance of darkness that still mars the world. The season is called Advent--the preparation for the celebration of Christ's birth, bringing with it new life in the deadness of winter.

For hundreds of years, God's garden--his people--thrived only to die again: "You brought us from Egypt as we were a tender vine;... You cleared the ground for us, and we took root and filled the land... But now... The boar from the forest devours us, and the wild animals feed on us... Turn us again to yourself, O Lord God Almighty" (Psalm 80:8, 9, 12, 19). For centuries the Hebrew people looked to a time when they would once again be "a well-watered garden" (Isaiah 58:11). And then, quite sudden-like, but by no surprise to the Eternal Eye, in the "fullness of time, God sent forth his son" (Galatians 4:4-5), a light shining "in the darkness" (John 1:5), and for those who believe the Christ-story, a new light and life in the midst of the darkness and the deadness.

Beneath the surface, the mulch had been prepared for the birth of something new and vibrant.

I know, it's only a vegetable garden, after all, and maybe it's not necessary to bring God into it. But as the sun sets so gently on the horizon, I stand in the middle of my garden and remember a greater light that shines the way to more wonderful things: a life grounded in the hope of a brighter tomorrow--a day filled with the abundance of all that is new, and good, and everlasting.

All because a child was born in Bethlehem some 2000 years ago.

Imagine that: All this, in a simple garden-variety birth...

... of the miraculous kind.

Surviving Christmas in a blended family--December 19, 2011

Christmas can be tough, especially for blended families. And apparently there are plenty of them. It's been estimated that more than half of Americans live in some form of a blended family. Stepfamily therapist, Steven Straub, believes that the blended family will become, if it's not already, the predominate family structure in the United States.

One of the major stressors during the holiday season involves the dynamics involved in blending a family. The holiday season comes packaged with enough tension already, what with gifts to buy, traffic to fight, and programs to attend. When you throw in the jealousies of a step grandmother, or the vengefulness of an ex-spouse, or the hurt feelings of stepchildren, or the insecurity of stepsiblings, (the variables for family strife are virtually endless) a veritable boiling cauldron of emotions threatens to spill over into the dream of the quaint family Christmas, scalding any possibility of what peace and joy might have been.

Eight years ago I experienced my first Christmas with our blended family. With each Christmas our family has drawn closer as together we've experienced the challenge of each holiday.

I've learned a few lessons that have helped me grow with my blended family during the holiday season.

I ceased chasing that perfect Christmas; it doesn't exist; there never was one and never will be. God could have made that first Christmas a perfect one, but he didn't. No room was left in the inn; and the holy family was homeless. Maybe God was trying to tell us something: Life is experienced in the struggle--in brokenness, in hurt, and in pain. Just as he was there in a dirty stable the first Christmas, so God is in the midst of our families' messiness.

Releasing the pressure of finding the perfect Christmas freed us to try new things. We've taken past traditions and incorporated them into our family in ways that created something different. For instance, we open some presents on Christmas Eve (a tradition from my family) and some on Christmas morning (a tradition in Lori's family), and in so doing started a new tradition.

I've also learned that no matter the number of children (we have four) in a blended family, each child is different, and each child is the same. Each has unique characteristics, but they all have the same basic emotional needs: love, acceptance, security, attention. In healthy family relations those needs can be met. Maybe that's why the biblical character, King David, described God as a "father to the fatherless, a defender of widows," a God who "places the lonely in families" (Psalm 68:5, 6).

Christmas season bristles with emotions so tense they sometimes seem to ricochet off the walls. I like the words of the Apostle Paul when he admonished his readers to "take care of those who are weak" (I Thessalonians 5:14). Often, during Christmas, those in blended families are experiencing the deep pain of broken relationships or feeling the emptiness of a loved one who is no longer there. Or maybe both.

It's perhaps the sense of loss--the absence of a parent or child at Christmas, the grief of what once was and never will be again--that is most pronounced in blended families. But, the void felt by changed circumstances cuts across the emotional landscape of all family structures, however "family" may be defined.

My mother and father are encountering the emotions experienced with their first Christmas in a retirement facility. "I miss the smells of cooking in my own kitchen, decorating my house, and inviting friends over," Mom confided to me the other day. And then with added insight, "One thing about it, life is about change, no matter your age or where you are."

Or the type of family you're in.

It's true; it's inevitable: Change is the permanent constant. Successfully blending a family is only saying, "Yes," to the possibilities for new life, knowing that whether it's Thanksgiving, Christmas, or Easter, life is found in the One who never changes, the One who calls us forward, the One who knows blending our life with those we love is what life is all about.

"All I want for Christmas is my nip and tuck" --December 2011

Back in 1944, while teaching music in public school, Donald Gardner asked his second grade class what they wanted for Christmas. Noticing how almost all his students answered him with a lisp because they had at least one front tooth missing, Gardner sat down and wrote the song, "All I Want for Christmas is My Two Front Teeth."

Unfortunately, at least for many youth, it takes much more than two new front teeth to fit into the norm physically; it takes a nip here and a tuck there.

Many, if not most, adults get cosmetic surgery because they don't want to look their age; they don't want to look like the rest. They want to be noticed in the crowd.

What's interesting is that the increase in teenagers getting cosmetic surgery (cosmetic surgical procedures on youths 18 and younger more than tripled from 1997- 2007, with the controversial procedures, breast augmentation and liposuction, increasing six fold) appears to be for the opposite reason adults choose plastic surgery. In a report by Camille Sweeney in *The New York Times*, Dr. Frederick Lukash, a cosmetic surgeon in New York City who specializes in treating adults, said, "Unlike adults who may elect cosmetic surgery for the 'wow' factor to stand out in a crowd, to be rejuvenated and get noticed, kids have different mantra. They do it to fit in."

Undergoing surgery to fit in is not without risks, risks most teenagers don't think through." Teenagers are often oblivious to the well-documented long-term health consequences of smoking, tanning, and other risky behaviors, and are likely to pay less attention to the risks of cosmetic surgery, making informed consent difficult," warns psychologist and women's health expert, Dr. Diana Zuckeman.

That's not to say all corrective surgery is wrong. On the contrary, some cosmetic procedures have worked wonders for a child's self-esteem. Michael Laudiso, now an adult, reported to Camille Sweeney that having his large ears pinned when he was ten was a life saver: "That surgery made me free."

Neither is there anything awry or unusual with trying to improve how we look or taking measures to look younger. Jane Fonda decided to go under the knife when she walked by a mirror, caught a glimpse of herself and wondered who that face belonged to. "I thought, 'Oh my God, it's me,'" Fonda told TODAY's Matt Lauer earlier this month. "I just decided I wanted to buy myself some time and look more like how I feel." said Fonda. She had work on her chin, neck and under the eyes.

But, the real danger lies when we adults create a cultural environment where a young person thinks every tiny detail has to be picture perfect, and where we ourselves think it's necessary to undergo countless procedures to keep getting that "wow" effect.

We forget the inner beauty that lies much deeper than our aging skin, a beauty that can grow even more attractive with age, a beauty that can't be touched by a scalpel.

Apparently, Lauren Scruggs' beauty is more than skin deep. She's the 23 year-old model who walked into the propeller of a an airplane, fracturing her skull, severing her left hand, breaking her collar bone, injuring her brain, and causing extensive damage to her left eye. Her first spoken words after regaining consciousness were, "I love you." And, when Lauren used a mirror to see her face for the first time after the accident, her response was, "That's not that bad."

I thought of her words as I was getting my haircut the other day. Glancing in the mirror at myself, I noticed a new wrinkle here and some sagging skin there. "Who is that guy who seems to be getting older quicker than I thought he would," I thought. Then, with a hidden smile, I repeated Lauren's words to myself, "That's not that bad."

And thanking the Lord for the gift of life itself, I said it again, "No, not that bad at all."

Chapter Seven

Tragedies Matter

Earthquake, Voodoo, and Reverend Robertson--January 23, 2010

After an intense secondary tremor shook Port-au-Prince, it makes you wonder if maybe there is something, after all, to the Reverend Pat Robertson's conclusion that it's pay-back time for the Haitians, the earthquake being a consequence of the people's two hundred year old deal with the devil to oust the French from their land. But the truth is, even if an earthquake so epic that it swallows the entire country into oblivion strikes tomorrow, it won't change the fact the Robertson is wrong, dead wrong.

Here's what Reverend Robertson said: "Something happened a long time ago in Haiti... they were under the heel of the French, uh, you know, Napoleon the third and whatever... and they got together and swore a pact to the devil, they said, we will serve you, if you get us free from the Prince. True story." Well, not exactly. "(The) notion of a pact with the devil is basically an echo of an old colonial response to the successes of the 1790s Haitian revolution," says UCLA anthropologist Andrew Apter. According to Professor Apter, it may or may not be true.

But, even it were true, even if the Haitians made some sort of pact with voodoo spirits, it still would not change the fact that Robertson's comments are misdirected. The natural disasters that have plagued Haiti or any other country or people are not the actions of a retributive God intent on punishing his creatures for actions that took place centuries, decades, or a few days ago. Hurricane Katrina, tornados in Kansas, and more recently a monster snow storm in the Mid-Atlantic, draught conditions in Alaska, or mud slides in California are not a punishment for the fact that several of the United States' founding fathers were Deists and Theists, not Christians.

It is, of course, the enormity of the tragedy that grabs us and begs for explanation. Had only three people died from the earthquake in Haiti, it would have been news in our homes for one evening only, a minor tragedy somewhere else, minor unless you were that mother whose only child was one of the three, or whose dad was one of the three, or whose brother was one of the three. It's only when we ourselves are hurt in some deep way, or we see many people in pain, or someone we love is grieved, only then do we ask "Why?" And then we demand from Someone an answer. We have no need of such when we have it under control. A toothache (a major cause of death in the Middle Ages) is no longer a matter of grave concern for us but only a mere inconvenience, which in most cases is alleviated by a quick call to the dentist, not a cry of "Why?" to a God who is judging me for a wrong I committed ten years ago. A direct correlation simply does not always exist between past sin and present suffering.

Job's friends played the "your pain is the result of your shady past" tune thousands of years ago; it was inadequate then, just as it is now.

But here we are, holding our guilt-cards close to our chest, hoping we won't have to lay them on the table for all to see, praying those indiscretions won't come back around, revealing our cheatin' heart, waiting, fearing, that an earthquake, or storm, or life-threatening illness will expose our backroom bargain with Mr. Devil.

If only Rev. Roberts were right, we could rest assured that our good behavior would keep us from disaster and earthquakes, and thunderstorms, and strep throat, skinned knees, and even bad grades, indeed, my Sweet Lord, from anything less than a full and meaningful life. Ahh yes! How we yearn for the moral certainty that $A + B$ always $= C$.

If it's true for an earthquake, it's true for whatever bad comes into your life. We live in an imperfect world where children stray, parents abuse, spouses cheat on each other, young mothers get cancer, breadwinners lose jobs, and yes, sometimes our pain is our own fault, but no, not always.

Life is messy, indeed. And suddenly there we are in our own Tsunami, or Katrina, or Haitian earthquake.

And we ask God, "Why?" And he answers with himself. No explanation necessary. Just ask Job.

Faces of Hope in the Tears of Tucson--January 10, 2011

You see their faces splashed on television: the victims of that horrible crime, the murders in Tucson. For just a moment we had been enjoying the cheerful news of good fortune in the life of Ted Williams--the once homeless man whose golden voice captured the internet and who now is inundated with golden offers, including a five second appearance in a Super Bowl commercial--when suddenly the images of Ted's smile were replaced by pictures of tears in Tucson. The sad irony of the Tucson tragedy is that so many faces of hope--smiling, optimistic, and buoyant faces--were instantly, maliciously attacked by the face of despair and the hand of hate.

And in that second it takes for a tear to fall, life can change forever.

By now you know of the youngest victim: nine year old Christina-Taylor Green. Christina-Taylor, with her big brown eyes, long brown hair, and innocent smile, arrived at the parking lot of Safeway in hopes of meeting one of her heroes, U.S. Representative Gabrielle Giffords. Christina-Taylor never got the chance. Ironically, Christina-Taylor's life was framed by tragedy: She was born on a tragic day--September 11, 2001--and died on another tragic day, January 8, 2011. Christina-Taylor was one of the 50 children featured in the book, Faces of Hope, representing babies born on 9/11. And a face of hope she was, even on 1-08-11.

Another victim, U.S. District Judge John Roll, was a widely respected federal judge and public servant. He was also a grandfather who was simply shopping at the Safeway where the shooting took place and walked to speak a kind word to Giffords. He owned a tender and gentle smile that evoked a sense of confidence and trust from others. John Roll--another face of hope in the tears of Tucson.

Rep. Giffords was meeting with voters outside the grocery store. "It's not surprising that today Gabby was doing what she always does, listening to the hopes and concerns of her neighbors," President Obama said of her. Her smile exudes optimism, courage, and strength coupled with humility. Her warm and inviting smile is yet another face of hope in the tears of Tucson.

And the alleged gunman who went after Giffords, the mentally unstable college drop-out, Jared Lee Loughner, had a smile… but not one of hope. Steven Rayle, a former ER doctor, was there. He had come to meet Giffords. What did he see in Loughner? A young man with a blank expression on his face. "I looked up and saw a man with a gun shoot her (Giffords) in the head and then continue firing, rapid-fire, with just point blank at everybody who was in the area."

When did this young man lose hope and turn to violence? We may never know. But he was not, at least at one time, beyond feeling the pain of isolation. In an interview with Clarence Williams of the *Washington Post*, Loughner's friend Timothy Cheves recalled a conversation with Loughner in which Cheves encouraged him to get his life on the right track. "I was telling him about God and all that. And he broke down, crying, and he gave me a big ol' hug, and said, 'Thank you, you're one of the only ones that ever listened to me.'"

And then, it happened. In the second it takes for a tear to fall, life can change forever. And beautiful faces, full of hope, are no more.

We want an explanation for the unexplainable; we want to find meaning in the senseless; we seek reasons in unreasonableness. And it's not there.

Sometimes all there is to do is let the tears fall. And enjoy the bit of life we are given, recalling those faces of hope that have graced our journey. And in the remembrance of them, be one, too, because in the second it takes for a tear to fall, life can change forever.

An Act of God? --March 16, 2011

> "Frightening beyond belief. I have no words."
> -Resident of Sendai, Japan, victim of the tsunami

Most of us who saw the telecasts of the tsunami's destruction in Japan could understand that man's reaction to the horror of the cataclysmic event. Your jaw drops. Your eyes widen. You have no words.

The devastation in Japan was so enormous---it's beyond words. In Minami Sanriku, a town in northeastern Japan, it's estimated that 9,500, people--half the town's population--may be unaccounted for. The death toll in Japan has exceeded10, 000. Multiple nuclear meltdowns threaten thousands more. Japan's prime minister said it is the nation's gravest disaster since World War II. In the words of President Obama, it is "heartbreaking."

The question inevitably edges in somewhere between the televised reports of the heartache and pain, between the visuals and the commercials, between the interviews and analyses, just as it did in other major natural disasters--whether it's Hurricane Katrina in 2005, the 2008 cyclone in Myanmar, or the 2010 earthquake in Haiti --the question arises and begs an answer, "Where is God in all this?" Where indeed? Why does God allow natural disasters like tsunamis, typhoons, tornados, earthquakes, and hurricanes?

The question is not only reserved for the monster sized disasters. Yesterday morning while updates of the tsunami were being broadcast on television, my wife received a text messaged prayer request. A friend of hers has a relative whose two day old baby is undergoing open heart surgery.

Included in the message were the heartfelt words, "I can't help but wonder how and why this is a part of God's plan."

Anyone who has felt the fear of loss and the agony of grief can empathize with the words in that text message. Even Job, righteous as he was, asked the question. Having been slammed to the canvas of life's tragedies, having lost everything except a nagging wife, he wanted to know why and just what in the heck he had done to deserve it. Is this pain of ours a result of random chance or an act of God? Rather than giving Job an answer, God revealed himself to him. And, in the presence of God, all Job could do was place his hand over his mouth.

Which is another way of saying, our question of who is responsible is unanswerable.

Nature itself, the apostle Paul tells us, is fallen, waiting for complete redemption. We can study nature and point to reasons for natural disasters. Hurricanes can be traced to warm waters and gale force winds, tsunamis are caused by underwater earthquakes, earthquakes are caused by the earth's shifting plates, and there is, I'm sure, a medical explanation for what caused the infants' heart problem.

The question on our minds is, why didn't God do something? Why didn't he direct Hurricane Katrina to some harmless place in the Gulf of Mexico? Why didn't he divert the earthquake in Haiti to an obscure place? Why didn't he take that tsunami into an unpopulated area in the middle of the Pacific? And why didn't he intervene in the life of the baby, preventing that heart problem from ever occurring? After all, he is God, isn't he? Isn't he in charge?

And the answer is yes, God is God. And at the same time, we live in this world and not another. The hurricane that died in the middle of the ocean doesn't make news, the tsunami that rocked the middle of the Pacific where no people live is a five second report on the Weather Channel, and God isn't questioned when the baby is healthy. God is rarely mentioned in those instances.

In the world we live in, it is inevitable that we will experience disasters. It's the natural order of things, and for God to intervene in every unsavory instance of our life would place us in a different world altogether. As C. S.

Lewis wrote in his classic work, *The Problem of Pain*. "Fixed laws, consequences unfolding by causal necessity, the whole natural order, are at once the limits within which (our) common life is confined and also the sole condition under which any such life is possible. Try to exclude the possibility of suffering which the order of nature and the existence of free wills involve, and you find that you have excluded life itself."

It's the world we live in; it's life itself, painful and tragic as it is.

It's an act of God.

When Steeples Fall--June 6, 2011

Two old codgers from Kansas decided to make a trip to California. On the way, they stopped at the Grand Canyon. Staring down at the Colorado River 6,000 feet below, gazing at the far side of the Canyon 18 miles away, awestruck by the canyon's multi-colored layers of rock, the two men stood speechless. Finally, one drawled, "Sumthun musta happened here."

Yep. It took several million years, but something indeed happened there. And it's a beautiful display, many would say, of God's handiwork in nature.

If you could have flown several hundred feet over Tuscaloosa, Alabama, or Joplin, Missouri, or Monson, Massachusetts, the day after tornadoes struck their cities with devastating force, you could have joined the old timer's declaration of the obvious: "Something must have happened here."

But unlike the gradual formation of the awe-inspiring beauty of the Grand Canyon, it took only a few minutes to wreak havoc in Tuscaloosa, Joplin, and Monson. And it was horrible.

We observe the creation of the Grand Canyon and stand amazed at how God put it together; we look at the tornado's destructive path and wonder if God went to sleep on the clock.

Tornadoes descend from the sky with strike force efficiency, destroying hospitals, high schools, and homes.

And houses of worship, too.

Harmony Heights Baptist Church in Joplin was hit by the tornado on Sunday, May 22, 2011, killing three women. Pastor Charlie Burnett believes it could have been much worse. "It has to be from God," Burnett said. Fifty people walked away from the church "when it looked like they should have died."

More than one church was hit by the tornado that trounced Alabama on April 27, 2011. Among those churches was the First Assembly of God in Pleasant Grove. Pastor Lamar Jacks tried to make some sense of it, "I don't understand it," Jacks said. "If I try to tell you I understand it, I'm lying. God's saying to us, do you trust me? Don't lean on our own knowledge. Just trust in him. God can take the bad and the hurts and lift up his name."

And in Monson, Massachusetts, Pastor Robert Marrone, on June 5, 2011, the Sunday morning after the storm hit his community, was also trying to make sense of it all. In his sermon, he asked where God was during the storm, "Did he take a break between 4 and 6?"--the time the tornado struck Massachusetts. It knocked down the steeple and severely damaged the historic church he pastors. But, Marrone saw evidence of God at work shortly after the storm. People began checking on and helping each other.

The technical term for these explanations is a theodicy--an attempt to defend the goodness and justice of God in the face of evil and suffering. If God is good, why does he allow tornadoes to strike buildings with people in them? It's one thing for him to permit a gradual transformation in creating something beautiful like the Grand Canyon. But what to do with a Tuscaloosa, a Joplin, or a Monson?

Somewhere between a view that attributes all suffering to a capricious God who uses natural tragedies as a way of punishing people--a God who destroys one house while leaving another intact, a God who grabs one baby from one mother's arms while leaving another alone--somewhere between that and the view that pain and suffering is somehow an area God didn't quite "fix" in his universe, lie the words of Jesus, who himself, although he never turned down someone in need of help, including healing, did not rush in, constantly intervening in the course of natural laws.

In speaking of who is responsible for tragedies, either from the hands of ruthless rulers or in construction accidents, Jesus made it clear it was not the result of wrongdoing on the part of the victims. Then warning his audience, Jesus said, "Unless you repent, you too will all perish" (Luke 13:3).

In other words, make sure you are straight with God, for you know not when the steeple may fall in your life.

So maybe we don't need to defend God. After all, he doesn't explain himself. And if he did, who of us could comprehend it all? Rather than giving an explanation, God gives himself.

Whether it's in the breathtaking view of the Grand Canyon or the heart-wrenching tragedy of destroyed buildings and lost lives, God is somehow there--in us--helping us respond to the beauty of the canyons or the beast of the calamities.

When steeples fall, he is there.

Even when words are beyond explaining how or why.

"Say it ain't so, Joe"--November 11, 2011

When I first heard the news of Joe Paterno's failure to do more to protect the kids in the case of Jerry Sandusky's alleged crime, my first thought was, "Say it ain't so, Joe"--the line the little boy supposedly spoke to baseball legend Shoeless Joe Jackson as he walked down the steps of the courthouse after appearing before a grand jury for allegedly fixing the 1919 World Series.

Conspiring to throw a ball game for money, the accusation--never proven--made to Jackson and seven of his teammates, may be shameful and tragic, but not doing more to stop a man who allegedly raped a 10 year old boy in a locker room shower is not just shameful and tragic, it's horrifying and disgusting.

The salaciousness of it, the manner in which it was overlooked, and the little ones who could have been saved from molestation--all this stunned a university and a nation.

Say it ain't so, Joe.

But unfortunately, it is so: "This is a tragedy," Paterno said. "It is one of the great sorrows of my life. With the benefit of hindsight, I wish I had done more."

Why didn't he? Why did a man who built what he called the "Grand Experiment,"--combining a championship football program with academic excellence--a man who built a career on the qualities of character and integrity and sought to instill those characteristics in his players--why, why didn't he do more?

The institution--in this case Penn State football--became bigger than life and in this instance protecting its life caused a terrible lapse in judgment. Paterno did what was legally required; he didn't do what was morally right. He shuffled the problem down the hall to the next administrative level and went back to work, recruiting, coaching, and winning. Success can be intoxicating, causing the best of people to rationalize or ignore wrong.

The success of an institution is never worth endangering the lives of children.

The comparison to what happened in the Roman Catholic Church can't be missed: Jonathan Mahler observed in *The New York Times*, "The parallels are too striking to ignore. A suspected predator who exploits his position to take advantage of his young charges. The trusting colleagues who don't want to believe it -- and so don't."

And so a pristine image is tarnished, an icon is shattered, a legend has fallen.

Previous to this terrible episode, Paterno spoke on ESPN of his legacy: "You coach when you're young to prove that you can do the job, and then there comes a point when you've got a family and you need to make a certain amount of dollars, and then there comes a point when the money's got nothing to do with it. It comes to a point where you say to yourself: 'What are you going to leave?'"

No one ever thought Joe Paterno would leave a mess behind him.

He has been condemned, and rightly so, for what he didn't do. But Paterno's life is not over. We should remember the words of historian James Anthony Froude, "The worth of a man must be measured by his life, not by his failure under a singular and peculiar trial."

Healing starts where last week's football game began: with the Penn State and Nebraska players kneeling together at midfield and praying for the victims in this tragedy. Remembering them will hopefully help prevent the further exploitation of children.

Joe will never be able to say it ain't so; his honor is tarnished. But perhaps in time he can find a way to speak words of healing and maybe remind those who loved him that despite his own failure of integrity, his team's motto, "success with honor," is still possible for leaders and followers. Indeed, this horrendous episode can underscore the need for constant vigilance in protecting the honor in all individuals, especially the weak and vulnerable.

Maybe someday Joe will have a voice again, but he will always walk with a painful limp as he tells the sad story.

The Unanswered Question in Theatre Number Nine—July 25, 2012

Why?

It's the first question I asked, and likely the one you first asked too.

It still echoes from theater number nine in the Century 16 Theatre in Aurora, Colorado, where 12 people were murdered and 58 injured.

And it's the one question we will never completely know.

We will in time learn the details of the hows: how he ordered the materials police say he used for the deadly booby traps found in his apartment; how he purchased the guns; how he so elaborately rigged his apartment with explosives and chemicals; and how he allegedly staged his murders. We may even learn how particular social and personal conditions led to his heinous act.

We are interested in those hows, but it's the why that eludes us.

Why would a brilliant, budding young scientist with a stellar academic record, a young man with no criminal history beyond a traffic violation, a student among the academically elite, working on his Ph.D. in neuroscience at the University of Colorado-Denver, why would he meticulously plan and carry out one of the most deadly crimes in U.S. history?

We feel better if we can find a reason. The media once again jumped to conclusions. Within hours of the massacre, ABC News' Brian Ross erroneously reported that a man with the same name as the suspect living in the same town was a member of the Colorado Tea Party. ABC promptly apologized.

Such efforts to politicize the murderous actions of a crazed man are futile attempts to answer the question, why.

We may feel better if we can find a reason for senseless acts of violence. And it's okay to ask why. It's our nature to ask why because we want a reason, a logical explanation for a senseless, meaningless act. We want to bring order to chaos. We somehow feel that if we can find an explanation for the evil, we can take measures to avoid it.

This murderous action reminds us that intelligence and academic achievement do not always equate with sanity or good moral judgment. An intelligent mind can be used for good or evil, according to how one chooses to use it. God is not a puppeteer. And evil by its very nature is senseless, opposing all that God is. We cannot always understand the why of evil. As the prophet Jeremiah wrote, "The heart is deceitful above all things and beyond cure. Who can understand it?" (Jeremiah 17:9).

Our unanswered question in no way diminishes God's presence among the grieving. Though we may walk through the valley of the shadow of death, surrounded by evil, God is still with us in our suffering and pain, even though the dark night may rise, momentarily extinguishing the light, and the pain may overwhelm, temporarily numbing our awareness of Him.

ABC News aired a video showing the suspect, James Holmes, speaking at a science camp at Miramar College in San Diego when he was 18. He gave a presentation on "temporal illusion," which Holmes defined as "an illusion that allows you to change the past." In the presentation, he says he studies subjective experience, which he says, "takes place inside the mind, as opposed to the external world."

Somewhere in time the reality of the external world and the illusion of his inner mind collapsed into a reign of terror.

Why? Was it a "temporal illusion... that allows you to change the past?"

Unfortunately it's not.

It's just evil.

Knowing there is no explanation for it, we lovingly embrace those closest to us as we call on God to bring hope to the hopeless and healing to the hurting.

Chapter Eight

Celebrating Life Matters

Capture the Present Moment This Year--January 23, 2009

Bad news has a way of traveling faster than good news; it has no respect for the number of a year; it bleeds through from one to another. The so-called "Santa Shooter" who murdered his ex-wife along with eight of her relatives on Christmas Eve is followed on New Years Day with the news of a man in Aspen, Colorado who delivered bombs wrapped as Christmas presents with a note threatening "mass death" if two banks did not turn over tens of thousands of dollars. We barely have time to say, "How crazy is that?!" than we hear of Hamas' launching of rockets into Israel. Now, Israeli ground troops have invaded Gaza. And this is just the violent side of bad news. What about the economy? Will it get worse before it gets better?

Maybe like me you shake your head in dismay. I find myself staring at my complimentary 2009 Norman Rockwell calendar and wondering, "What happened to that world? Was it ever?"

Yes and no. Go back and read the newspapers in Rockwell's day. Bad news was there too; bad news is generational. But Rockwell, whether you consider him an artist or merely an illustrator, had a knack for taking everyday life scenarios and depicting them on canvas. I am no artist. But even I know that any successful artist must be able to see what others miss. Somehow those seemingly common events are captured by the artist's eye.

So, instead of fantasying about bygone days or residing in a future that is not yet, why not see through the smoke created by evil forces beyond our control? Why not capture the good on the canvas of the soul? Why not this New Year declare yourself an artist of sorts, a spiritual artist, if you will?

And what could be a better subject for the spiritual artist than sensing the presence of God in everyday life? If we could see with spiritual eyes, really sense Him and His work, if we could know the presence of God in the here and now, we would rise above the bad to the very best of life. And it's not a "Rockwellesque" dream. It's the most real of all realities! It's the presence of God painted in and through your heart.

How? Just how does that happen?

A seventeenth century French Jesuit priest named Jean-Pierre de Caussade might be of help. De Caussade was appointed the spiritual director of a Jesuit retreat house where he undertook the spiritual direction for the Nuns there. They wrote down what he taught them, and years later those notes were published as a book, *The Sacrament of the Present Moment*. (If you teach, it's frightening to think your legacy could lie in the notes your students took!)

In essence what De Caussade taught was that God speaks to every individual through what happens moment by moment. Paring all down to the core of religious duty, he said, "There remains one single duty. It is to keep one's gaze fixed on the master one has chosen and to be constantly listening so as to understand and hear and immediately obey his will." How is this done? De Caussade said that "the only condition necessary for this state of self-surrender is the present moment in which the soul, light as a feather, fluid as water, innocent as a child, responds to every movement of grace like a floating balloon."

What a way to begin the New Year! How about this for a New Year's resolution: Live each moment in the presence of the Lord with the desire to obey his every command.

But what about the bad moments we will inevitably encounter this year? De Caussade was well aware of that, too. What could be worse than seeing your son crucified? De Caussade points to Mary, the mother of the Lord, as the example of how to apprehend the presence of God even in ugly circumstances: "When all the world disowned, abandoned and persecuted her son, she followed him from the stable to Calvary. In the same way faithful souls triumph over a succession of mortifications, shadows and fantasies which contrive to make God's purpose unrecognizable, and pursue and adore it to the very foot of the cross."

It is not always easy to find Him; His presence is easily missed. But the artist will persevere and even get better at finding Him. God is there. No, He is here... now... in each present moment of this and every year.

A Resolution Revolution--January 3, 2011

I resolve to stage a revolt against making New Year's resolutions. I've had it with them; they don't work for me. The New Year is still in infancy, and I've already broken 75% of my resolutions.

It's not that I didn't try; I just forgot: the pressure of the moment distracted my attention from keeping the resolution.

Take my first resolution, for example. I read that being impatient can lead to hypertension. I tend to be impatient, and I don't want hypertension. "Patience," I said to myself as I stood in line at the grocery store a couple of days before New Year's, tapping my foot as I wondered if the next line was moving faster, "patience is something I could work on." Thus, resolution number one: be more patient; don't sweat the small stuff.

Since Lori and I had already planned to be away during the New Year's holiday, I would have a nice, relaxed atmosphere to begin my first resolution. On the morning of January 1, I took my time as Lori and I casually walked to the breakfast buffet. I was silently complimenting myself on how well I was doing on resolution number one when Lori informed me she had forgotten the breakfast coupons--part of the weekend package with our hotel. "You forgot the coupons?" I grimaced.

That initial, suppressed grimace was followed by a bigger, more obvious one when the hostess told me there was a 45 minute waiting list and that I would have to check at the front desk about the possibility of reclaiming the breakfast vouchers. Glancing at the long line at the hotel registration desk, I grumbled to Lori, "I'll wait in line while you see if you can remember where you put the breakfast coupons." When Lori couldn't find them, I decided to conduct a thorough and proper search myself, and voila, I found them... in the cabinet on *my* side of the bed. "Oops." I kinda forgot I put them there.

So much for resolution number one.

Getting the proper amount of sleep, I have been told, is essential to our health. My 5-6 hours of sleep a night isn't adequate, I concluded. Thus, resolution number two: get more sleep. I proudly announced to Lori on New Year's Day--after apologizing for breaking resolution number one, of course--"I'm going to bed early tonight." That was a bold statement for me, and one I had to promptly retract when I remembered that my OU Sooners played in the Fiesta Bowl that very night and that the broadcast didn't begin until 8:30 p.m. (EST) So, there I was whooping and hollering my team to victory at 12:30 a.m. And preachers can't sleep in on Sunday mornings, you know.

So much for resolution number two.

Resolution number three: maintain a more healthy diet, went down with the New Year's breakfast buffet, as did resolution number four, cut back on my caffeine consumption. (Free refills came with the buffet, what was I to do?) I'm managing to chase resolution number five: read through the Bible again this year, although I'm already 8 chapters behind. Resolution number six: cash instead of credit--good, except for the gas card. Resolution number seven, journal each day--already days behind, although I have at least located my journal; resolution number eight: have a book proposal ready by March 1--I'm working on it. And number nine, read at least one hour a day--I'm on it. Resolution number ten--stop the nervous habit of picking my fingernails--was lost in the excitement of the OU game.

There you have it: as far as I can figure, I'm only hitting 250-300% on my resolutions.

But wait a minute: Isn't the highest career professional baseball batting average Ty Cobb's? And isn't his record a "mere" .366? That means that almost 60% of the time, when he stepped up to the plate, he didn't get a hit. And that's the best career average EVER.

So maybe I don't need to start a resolution revolution after all. Maybe the revolution I need is a continuation of the good in what I have resolved, not a cessation of the goal itself. As John Norcross, psychology professor at the University of Scranton in Pennsylvania said recently in *The Wall Street Journal*, "Keeping a resolution isn't a 100-yard dash. It's a marathon."

That's it: a marathon. In a marathon, I can get bumped to the side and even trip and fall and still get back up and finish the race in respectable fashion. And somehow in the running of the race, I can feel like a revolutionary, a revolutionary because I resolved to persevere, and even though I may finish with a limp, I nonetheless can cross the finish line, aiming for a goal far beyond 2011.

The Sad Side of Easter--April 28, 2011

My family followed traditional American Easter traditions, so when I was a child---in addition to preparing for the Sunday morning worship of the resurrected Christ---we anticipated the Easter event by dyeing Easter eggs for the family Easter egg hunt, sending Easter cards, and exchanging little chocolate Easter bunnies. Dad was a dentist and candy was generally discouraged in our house, so chomping down on one of those miniature chocolate Easter bunnies was a rare and unusual treat. (One year my older brother Mark was lucky enough to receive a life-sized chocolate bunny, not a tiny one--- but he was permitted to eat only one bunny ear on Easter day.)

Ahh---Easter, a very happy celebration of life.

It wasn't until years later that I came to know the sad side of Easter.

It came not at once but in a slow accumulation of events---beginning with the death of my brother, Dougie, my buddy, my playmate, my friend--- and the realization at age 6, that he wasn't coming back from up there in the sky, that death was permanent. It continued with other tragedies along life's way: the assassinations of John F., Bobby, and Martin Jr., ---- their murders marking the end of innocence--- grandmother's funeral, then another grandmother's funeral, and granddad too. Then my "happily ever after, I do," was followed after so many years, by the death of my wife--- and the subsequent massaging of grief in the lives of my two children who no longer had a mother.

Easter brought no one back, nor did it preserve life from other tragic events.

But neither was it meant to.

After all, Lazarus did at last die---once and for all.

The sad side of Easter is life before Easter, without Easter---life without the hope of Easter-life.

That means the road to Easter cannot be an easy one. Millions of Christians will celebrate Easter this Sunday. But to get there, they must go through Good Friday. And Good Friday is no walk in the park. At least it wasn't for the One who made it Good Friday. For him it was anything but good. The betrayal, the scourging, the crown of thorns, the leering crowds, the nails piercing his hands and feet, the spear in his side---that's not exactly a T.G. I. F. day.

Tragic events of life remind us that there is a sad side of Easter. It's real. And it's painful.

The recently released film, *Soul Surfer*, depicts that unpleasant truth in the life of surfing champion, Bethany Hamilton, whose left arm was ripped off in a shark attack in 2003, when she was 13 years old. Refusing to give up on her dream of becoming a professional surfer, Bethany learned to surf with one arm and went on to compete successfully.

But she struggled with why it happened; she burned with jealous feelings when she saw beautiful girls with pretty arms; she had to train hard to do what once came easily.

And she worked through it.

"God put me on earth to serve Him, and I know He's gone through so much worse things. I know that having one arm is the way He uses me. And I'm so happy," Bethany said in a 2006 interview.

When Bethany spoke of God going through so much worse than she had experienced, I assume she was talking about the suffering of Jesus--- something Christians observe this week in what is called Holy Week, which culminates with Jesus' death on Good Friday.

Good Friday is good only because of the bad that Jesus endured. I like the way cartoonist, Johnny Hart, put it in a poem he has one of his "B.C." cartoon characters write. Wiley sits under a tree and pens the words:

"When History has recorded it all/Events both happy and sad/Good Friday shall reign as the worst and the best/that mankind has ever had."

The worst and the best, the very same day, gave way to what Easter is: an invitation to life.

I think Bethany Hamilton would agree. And so would all of Jesus' followers--- at least those who know how the sad side of Easter can lead to its happy side, come Sunday morning.

Another earth, another you, another year--December 23, 2011

Scientists have finally discovered another earth. Well, sort of.

Earlier this month NASA's Kepler space telescope team announced the discovery of "Kepler-22b," located in what is called a "habitable zone," meaning an environment that's not too hot or too cold for the possibility of life. And just last week, the team unveiled two other earth-sized planets, Kepler-20e and Kepler-20f, although they are not in the habitable zone.

"This discovery shows that we Homo sapiens are straining our reach into the universe to find planets that remind us of home. We are almost there," said Geoff Marcy of the University of California, Berkeley, one of the world's leaders in the search for planets.

But apparently a lot of space exists between those two words, "almost," and "there." Being reminded of home and finding another earth is more than a world or an earth apart. Kepler-22b for instance, is 600 light years away. Traveling by space shuttle, it would take 22 million years to get there. And Kepler 22b's size, 2.4 times the size of earth, makes it too big for an atmosphere like earth's, according to planetary scientist Lena Noack.

Yet scientists are invigorated by the possibility of finding another earth: "You can bet that the hunt is on to find... a true earth twin," avers astronomer David Charbonneau of Harvard University.

Although I've never been a science fiction fan, the dreamer in me is fascinated with the concept of another earth and what it would be like.

The 2011 film, *Another Earth*, explored the idea of another earth as an opportunity for a second chance in life, a place where a parallel you exists with another, possibly better life. The producers used astrophysicist, Dr. Richard Berendzen, (author of *Pulp Physics*) for the background voice asking the probing questions about a parallel earth and our place in it: "Could we even recognize ourselves, and if we did, would we know ourselves? What would we say to ourselves? What would we learn from ourselves? What would we really like to see if we could stand outside ourselves and look at us?"

The truth is, we don't have to travel 22 million years in space to find a place where we can ask those or similar questions. Standing on the precipice of a New Year is occasion enough to step outside ourselves and take inventory of who we are, really.

Do we know what to say to ourselves? Do we know the self to whom we speak? Are we strangers to ourselves?

C.G. Jung, the Swiss psychoanalyst, wrote about an inner dimension he referred to as the True Self. For Jung, this Self, as author Sue Monk Kidd points out, doesn't refer to the ego, as in myself, but to the Center of our being, the image of God within us. As we find and cultivate that place we discover our True Self.

It's the place Jesus of Nazareth described as being, "The Kingdom of God within you" (Luke 17:21), and when we reject it, we also deny our True Self. As Thomas Merton, the Trappist monk of Gethsemani Abby said, "My false and private self is the one who wants to exist outside the reach of God's will and God's love...And such a self cannot help but be an illusion." For Merton, the secret of our identity, our True Self, is "hidden in the love and mercy of God."

Sometime between now and the New Year, I think I'll step outside and peering into the universe, ponder the possibility of another earth, and then, I'll look within, and even though I'm not there--still without all the answers--I'll find comfort in the words of the young theologian, Dietrich Bonhoeffer, who before being martyred by the Nazis, concluded his poem, "Who Am I?" with the line, "Whoever I am, Thou knowest, O God, I am Thine!"

Knowing the same One who has me also has the universe and all that's in it, I'll then say "Yes," to my True Self, and taking God's hand, step boldly into another New Year.

Only pictures on a calendar?--January 8, 2012

The New Year already has flown, leaving its newborn status lying flat in the nest.

And I'm left with all these extra calendars--two from local businesses, two from churches which somehow think I will be interested in adding their agenda to my schedule, and another complimentary calendar from a company wanting me to buy calendars to give people next year, assuming, I suppose, that I somehow believe others will be interested in my agenda next year.

But I like the pictures on these calendars, anyway.

Most appealing to me are calendars with pictures of nature coinciding with each season, which is nice, especially if you live in a place where you don't have distinct seasons. In Oklahoma, where I grew up, we could have a brutal winter followed by a miserably hot summer--both of which seemed to endure forever. But fall was a weekend fling, and spring was a whiff in the air. So I loved gazing into those calendar pictures of the New England fall foliage or a radiant springtime in Kentucky. Ahh--how relaxing they seemed, especially to a high strung high school kid.

Why do so many calendars have pictures of animals--dogs, cats, horses? I suppose if petting a dog or having a cat curl up in your lap can steady your emotions on a roller coaster day, maybe the next best thing would be a picture of a likeable creature. And that's nice, especially when so many of the human species aren't.

Calendars with mountain or ocean scenes can bring relief from the harsh realities of life, too. Just imagine you are there, and that can smooth wrinkled emotions.

But, of all the calendars I enjoy, one calendar stands above all the rest.

That's happens to be the custom calendar my wife created online. Each month is filled with pictorial memories of my family. I turn to January and there is Mary and me, having a cup of Community Coffee in the kitchen; in April Lori is baking a birthday pie for Madi; I look to July and there's Dave and Madi splashing in the pool with our two Schnauzers; a glance at August and Mary and Madi are cooking an Italian dish for grandparents; and finally, I'm in December smiling at Harrison opening presents.

Relax, release, rejuvenate.

Calendar pictures of family soothe me amidst the stress and strain of life, reminding me, as I close my eyes with those pictures in my mind's eye, of life's priorities. Unlike the old flip books, which created an illusion of motion as you thumbed through them, glancing through the calendar's family photos does quite the opposite: It halts the movement into a single photo shot, a sort of mental composite, leaving us with an image of what's really important: family.

I've never known anyone in their dying moment wish for more time at the office. But I have seen, time and again, person after person, finding comfort as they lay dying in the presence of their family.

Death brings the living together--at least for a dying moment.

On this calendar day, I'm standing with a young couple at the graveside service for their stillborn child. Grieving the memories of memories that never happened--their baby's first cry, the giggles, the words "Dada," and "Mama," the baby's first steps--the parents seem mesmerized by the tiny box containing the body of their baby.

Having closed the service, the harsh January wind whips across our faces as I ask: "Would you like a little time here just to yourselves, apart from the rest of your family?"

"No," the father whispers, "we can only make it as a unit."

A unit--a family unit.

I doubt that cemetery scene will be on a calendar picture next year or ever, but I hope the words will echo for that family through the months of each year: "We can only make it as a unit."

Death is a part of living, and though it's usually an uninvited and unwelcomed guest, it still intrudes onto our calendars without our invitation or embrace, reminding us that it has an appointment with each of us on a number somewhere between one and thirty-one. But the family pictures, those memories of life--or even the desire for it--breathe significance into what is past and cast hope for the future: We can make it as a unit, a family unit.

And that's the truth--no matter what pictures are on your calendar.

Correcting our failure to communicate this Easter--April 4, 2012

George Bernard Shaw once said, "The single biggest problem in communication is the illusion that it has taken place." Communication is an imperfect science, to say the least.

I picked up the phone just the other day and thought I correctly read the caller ID: "Lebanon Elementary School," the school where my wife works. So naturally, I assumed it was her.

But that's not what it said. And it wasn't her.

I didn't have my reading glasses on, and though I held the phone at arm's length and squinted, I still missed the name.

But, convinced it was Lori, I blurted, "Hey, Babe, why didn't you call me on my cell, like you always do?"

I could feel tension on the other line, then a timid, "Could I speak with Lori?"

Oops. It definitely wasn't Lori.

Then I wrongly assumed it was another teacher: "Oh, I'm sorry," I chuckled, a bit chagrined at the thought of how I had referred to the caller as "Babe."

I tried to recover: "You want to speak with Lori? But Lori's with you isn't she?"

"No, sir, Lori isn't with me."

"Then where is she?" I asked with confusion oozing from my voice.

Now, with the faintest hint of irritation, "Sir, I'm calling to confirm her appointment tomorrow."

Ahh, I finally got it, even without my reading glasses.

I wished I hadn't answered the phone and just let the voice mail get it. I imagined the receptionist hanging up the phone, twirling her seat around, and giggling to her co-workers. The whole thing had probably been recorded for quality control.

"Hey, come on over here and listen to this guy," I could hear her saying as she bent over in her chair laughing. The whole office is now primed for a funny one before they even hear my voice. I could see them all gathered around the recorder, laughing hysterically till their sides ache.

"We needed that," one chortles.

"Talk about a confused hubby," says another.

They shake their heads in pity at me as they return to work.

Having located my reading glasses, I try and dismiss this scene by calling my 87 year-old father. Sharing my embarrassing moment with him will be cathartic, I think. But first I ask him how he's doing.

"Ok, now," he says, "but yesterday we saw the worst movie ever." (Dad and a group of men at his retirement center go to a movie once a week.) "Foul language, horrible. I don't know why people think they have to talk like that. And this couple lived together just to have sex. Terrible."

"Well, what was the name of the movie?"

"I don't even know."

"You didn't know the name of the movie? Why did you see it?"

"Didn't intend to. We misread the marquee and went in the wrong theatre!"

I started laughing at the thought of these perplexed men, well into their 80s, sitting in the wrong theater, grimacing at each other, trying to figure out what's going on.

Then, I caught myself. "What am I laughing about? I haven't told him *my* story."

As the saying goes, "The acorn didn't fall far from the tree."

And if you think about it, it didn't fall far from you either.

We're all communicatively impaired. The Tree of Communication Confusion, planted in the Garden of Eden, blossomed when our first ancestors ignored God and misread Satan. Then the confusion went viral at the Tower of Babel. Though down the centuries, through word and prophesy, God kept trying to grab humankind's attention, most just didn't get it.

As a last resort that was always in the works, God himself came in the flesh to talk like one of us in our language.

"Anyone with ears to hear should listen and understand" (Mark 4:9), Jesus said. But even after the resurrection of Christ, it was difficult to read the message, at least at first sight: "It was Jesus, but she didn't recognize him" (John 20:14), John noted of a disoriented Mary Magdalene.

But it's a true and wonderful story, even though we still struggle to understand, and this week Christians celebrate it---the Passion of Christ, culminating in his death and resurrection.

So, put your reading glasses on and find the right theater. You don't want to miss this one.

Chapter Nine

Life Lessons Matter

Back it Up--March 3, 2010

I stood before the computer tech with my laptop in both hands, as if I were offering my firstborn into her care. "Dr. David, have you backed up your documents?" she asked.

I shamefully lowered my head, guilty again. "No," I answered. I could hear the words of my son, Dave, echoing in the background of my mind: "Dad, how many times do I have to show you how to back up your documents? How is it that you can explain Blaise Pascal's writings on faith and reason, and you can't remember how to back up your documents? I just don't get it." I didn't either, that's why I fail to back up my documents. (I have since learned you can go online and receive instructions on how to backup your computer using an external hard drive, called a flash drive.) But now I was in trouble. My computer had crashed, and the hard drive was scrambled, which meant it had to be replaced. And worst of all was the news Kaylene Poff, my website manager and computer tech, broke to me, "If you don't have it backed up, it could be lost. I hope we can save it."

"Lost, as in vanished, irretrievable, gone… forever?" I hesitatingly asked.

My mind reeled, recalling just a few of the documents I not backed up: at least three chapters (I couldn't' remember, it may have been more, I was too embarrassed to entertain the thought) of a manuscript I have been working on, numerous sermons, articles I have submitted, scripts of radio messages, syllabi, exams, poems I had written, not to mention pictures only in my possession--the picture of my son's high school football team kneeling in prayer after a game, Lori and me on the beach, Lori and me in our garden.

At this point, I anticipated a deep, dark, foreboding funk overshadowing my future as I recalled a story from my days at Princeton Seminary. Dr. J. Christiaan Beker, Professor of New Testament Theology, was, or so the story goes, on a train in Germany with his doctoral dissertation in hand. He got off the train, realized he had left his dissertation on board, rushed back, only to find it was too late: The dissertation was gone. Beker supposedly descended into a deep depression, and it took him years to come out of it and redo his doctoral thesis.

Then there is author and Professor of Creative Writing, Andrew Porter, who came home from work one day to discover thieves had stolen his computer, briefcase, and disks containing everything he had ever written. After trying unsuccessfully to rewrite his material, he left his agent, sought another career, and didn't write another word for three years.

Losing pieces of our work, which is a part of our life, easily extends beyond frustrating to depressing. The family pictures lost after a divorce, the scrapbook burned in the fire, the children's finger paintings left behind in the fifth move, the love notes forgotten somewhere in the attic of another house---all remain in the recesses of our memory until we want them, and find... they're not there.

No retrieval. No recovery. No redemption.

My grandmother Whitlock's mind faded; I watched her memories of life disappear uncontrollably like letters on a word document being erased by a stuck delete button. Some things you can't backup. Life flashes like a comet into eternity, too quick, too ethereal to backup.

It's then that we have to trust those memories, the essence of our life, with the Someone to whom we pray will hold them securely in the eternal harddrive of the heavenlies.

"Good news, Dr. David. We were able to backup all your documents."

"Thanks, Kaylene... for now."

The Dark Side of Religion--April 30, 2010

Pastor Fred Phelps' God is mad. Phelps' God is mad at most everyone, except Phelps and his congregation, the Westboro Baptist Church in Topeka, Kansas. According to a press release on their website, GodHatesFags.com, a group from the church was scheduled to picket outside the church I pastor in Lebanon, Ky. But, they travel far beyond Kentucky; Phelps and his gang may be coming to your neighborhood soon. Why? Because at opportune times, the dark side of religion inevitably emerges.

Whenever a group within a religion so elevates one aspect of their belief system that those who don't adhere to it are depersonalized as "heathen" or "infidels," as "anathamas," or "fatwas," the dark side of religion becomes evident. While the possibilities for labeling are endless, the result is the same: The unbeliever becomes a non-person, an object, a "thing" to be hated, ridiculed, bullied. Given the right political and social circumstances, religious people can in the name of God, commit acts of hate, violence, torture, and even murder.

Most of us associate this dark side of religion with fanatical Islam. But it is possible in any religion, including Christianity. It's history bears this out: from the Crusades and Inquisition of the Middle Ages, to John Calvin's Geneva, where Micahael Servetus was executed in 1553 for his anti-Trinitarian views, to radical aspects of the Anabaptist movement of the 16th century, such as, for example, Jan van Leiden's religious dictatorship in Munster, Germany, resulting in the besieging of the city and the deaths of many. And Christianity had yet to arrive in North America. All this in the name of religion.

Fred Phelps and his followers prove the dark side of religion is still alive and well, and is as dark as ever.

Emphasizing that God chooses some people for salvation and some for damnation, then exalting this belief above all others, Phelps identifies the "damned" with the United States, claiming this nation is the modern day equivalent of Sodom and Gomorrah. Why? Because The United States tolerates Gay people and even has laws protecting them as citizens. Phelps, by the way, prefers to call Gays, "Fags," because faggots will burn them in hell, hence the title of his website.

Because he believes God is mad at the United States, it makes perfect sense to Phelps that whenever an American soldier is killed in action, it's because God is taking out his wrath on a nation that doesn't prosecute homosexuals as outlaws. But Phelps believes God's anger is not reserved for soldiers who protect this godless nation of ours; God orchestrates other tragic events to make his point. For example, in a sermon preached on April 21, 2010, Phelps maintains that the recent coal mining tragedy in West Virginia in which 29 workers died is an example of what he calls, "GodSmacks." And true Christians are to rejoice when God smacks this nation in violent ways.

And that's why they threatened to picket outside our church, Lebanon Baptist, in Lebanon, Ky., this past Sunday. It was the funeral service for Sergeant Randy S. Segley, Jr., a member of my congregation, who had served his country until his death in Afghanistan. Sgt. Segley was remembered as an honorable man, a friend of many, a decorated soldier. His parents, who wept during the service, were praised as having raised Randy well.

None of that matters to the protestors of Westboro Baptist Church. It is their practice to hold signs for grieving families to see as they exit the funeral. Signs that say: "You're Going to Hell"; "God Hates Fags"; "God Hates the U.S.A." And, with their children usually standing in front of them, the religious picketers denounce the deceased. According to Mike Sexton, Central Kentucky's Ride Captain for the Patriot Guard, an organization that attempts to shield fallen soldiers' families from the Westboro Baptist members, a typical vituperation is "God bless the I.E.D. (Improvised Explosive Devise) that killed your son."

It's theology gone bad; the dark side of religion.

The Patriot Guard lined the outside of our church, ready to shield the family as they left for the graveside; the Guard held flags; the motorcycles they had driven to the funeral were close by, ready for them to start and drown the religious hecklers' voices.

But the Westboro Baptists didn't show this time. "Probably because it wasn't televised, and this is a smaller community. They do like publicity," Sexton, a native of Richmond, Ky., whispered to me. And then he added, "This is their practice: they threaten to show, and we always have to be ready; you never know which funeral they'll be at."

I sighed with relief. And as the casket passed my way, the irony hit me like a flash of lightning: here we have soldiers fighting and dying for the freedom of a nation that allows the dark side of religion to exist--along with a religious right and a religious left, homosexual people and "straight" people, fundamentalists and liberals, orthodox and the unorthodox. And I thanked God that I live in such a country.

And I wondered if somewhere deep down in the darkness, Phelps might too.

The Curious Case of Aaron Glascock--May 13, 2010

Daisy: "You're so young."
Benjamin Button: "Only on the outside."
---from *The Curious Case of Benjamin Button*

Time is slipping away for Aaron Glascock. It daily slithers through his fingers, snakes unseen through the iron bars that keep Aaron confined, clandestinely floats by the security doors at the Federal prison's entrance, and happily rises to freedom, leaving Aaron behind, stuck in a past he can't reclaim, aging ever so quickly, growing older from the inside out.

Aaron's youthful, twentyish-looking face, fit, athletic build, and boyish grin betray an inner age far beyond his 33 years. Now eleven years into a thirty year sentence for conspiracy to distribute cocaine, Aaron, native of Lebanon, Ky., and member of the church I pastor, remains hopeful that somehow, someway, his sentence will be commuted. Federal law requires that he serve at least 85% of his sentence. He will be 48 years old when he is released. Aaron's last great hope is that President Barack Obama will commute the sentence to time served.

His case is curious in many ways and points to inconsistencies in the federal judicial system.

How is it that a young man in his early twenties, a law-abiding, church-going, well-rounded young man with a steady girlfriend, a young man who was a model pre-med student, a biology major at an academically respected Catholic school, Bellarmine University, how is it that he, in his last semester before graduating, gets charged with conspiracy to traffic in drugs? Perhaps the answer lies in a young man's desire for a father's relationship.

In the spring of 1998 Aaron's father, who had not been a part of his son's life for years, suddenly took an interest in him. He began taking Aaron, by then a college student at Bellarmine, to Florida when Aaron was on spring or summer break. His father was supposedly buying homes, making needed repairs, and selling them at a profit. Aaron would help with electrical wiring. He liked staying in a beach-front hotel and hanging out at the beach. He didn't bother to ask where the money was coming from. Three such trips had been made when his father asked Aaron to do something curious: make a trip not to Hollywood, Florida, their usual destination, but to Gainesville, Florida, and travel not with his dad but with his father's friend. They were to start working on repairing homes until the elder Glascock could arrive.

The first night in Gainesville, early on the morning of March 11, 1999, officers with the Drug Enforcement Agency (D.E.A.) knocked on their hotel room door, burst in, read Aaron his rights, and charged him with trafficking in cocaine.

His life would never be the same. Time would pass, but Aaron would remain frozen in 1999, aching from within, holding on to his childhood dream of becoming a physician, slowly aging on the inside as his dream slowly faded until, like the early morning fog, it finally disappeared at high noon with the rejection of Aaron's third appeal.

Aaron could have admitted guilt and received 12 years, or he could have cooperated and been sentenced to 3 years. That was the "deal" the government offered him. He turned down both options, refusing the first, since he maintained he knew nothing and was therefore innocent; he would not cooperate, believing that justice would surely prove his innocence, allowing him to pursue his life-long dream: a medical career.

It's curious how at his first trial the judge first allowed two government witnesses who could have exonerated Aaron to testify, but during the court's recess, before the witnesses could speak, the judge suddenly without an explanation, rescinded the order permitting the witnesses to testify.

It's curious that the informant most deeply involved in the two year investigation of the drug ring testified that he had never seen, heard, or knew of Aaron Glascock.

It's curious that the primary testimony against Aaron came from three convicted criminals already in the county jail where Aaron was first incarcerated, testifying in exchange for a reduction in their sentence that Aaron had said he "knew what was going on."

It's curious, in light of Aaron's conviction, that the reputed leader of the drug smuggling enterprise, James Gregory Boswell, told government agents that "the kid," meaning Aaron, had no knowledge of the drug transactions.

That 30 year sentence is curious too, especially when you consider that it's longer than that given to Manuel Noriega, the former Panamanian dictator and drug smuggler, longer than the ten year sentence for conspiracy to murder given to John Walker Lindh (alias Sulayman al-Faris), who was captured by American soldiers as an enemy combatant in Afghanistan, and it's longer than the average amount of time actually served by first time sex offenders.

Curious? Indeed.

In prison, Aaron rests in Psalm 23, finds solace in Jesus' words that we are not to worry about tomorrow, and prays for mercy.

As I leave, walking through the prison gates, wondering if there are other Aaron Glascocks behind other prison walls, the wind hits my face, awakening me to the freedom on the outside; the setting sun's orange glow reminds me that another day is passing into infinity; and my heart cries for an explanation to a curiosity: how a man's soul--worn by the routine of prison life, wizened to the skill of prison survival, scorched by disappointment in the court system--can be aging so quickly and yet still be so alive, even as that burdened soul is hidden beneath a hopeful outlook, a warm handshake, and words that promise a new tomorrow.

People Are Work--February 14, 2011

"People are work, brother. A lot of work. Too much work." So said Detective Frank Keller (Al Pacino) a New York City detective in the 1989 movie *Sea of Love*. Keller had just solved an emotionally draining, life threatening, relationship changing investigation of a serial killer. In the movie, Keller falls in love with Helen Cruger (Ellen Barkin) who happens to be a main suspect in the case and doesn't know that Keller is an undercover detective. They begin a serious relationship, but she rejects Keller, who had just saved her life, because she felt deceived by him. The "people are work" quote comes close to the end of the movie, when Keller is venting his frustration in a bar to his friend and fellow detective Sherman Touhey, played by John Goodman.

On occasion I have echoed the Pacino quote. I can identify with the minister in the cartoon that shows him arriving home late for supper. When his wife asks him why he is an hour late, he replies, with a tired, bewildered look on his face, "I asked Mrs. Jones how she was doing."

People can be work indeed. And some people are as Pacino observed, "a lot of work." We all know those special folks who try our patience, push our buttons, and unravel our day. As Mme. de Stael said, "The more I see of man, the more I like dogs."

I recall my dad, a dentist, shaking his head late one Saturday night after a patient called him. Seems this man had a real emergency, a toothache that was unbearable. "And how long has it been bothering you?" Dad asked. "All week," the man replied. "But I just didn't have time to make an appointment earlier in the week, and now, I can't stand it, Doc. Can I meet you at your office now and get it pulled?" "Now," happened to be midnight.

People are work. The problem is, unless you are a hermit or a solitary scientist in a think tank somewhere, people are an unavoidable part of work. Without people, we have no work. That reminds me of the burned out school teacher who confessed, "I love teaching; it's just the students I can't stand."

So, what to do with those few—those ones who are "a lot of work," the minority whose voices cackle with the loudness of a majority, the small ones who can gulp huge portions of our time and attention?

Psychologists recommend sharing your frustration with someone you totally trust. That's what Pacino was doing. If you have no such person, get alone and shout it out. Let off some steam. And, as much as possible, don't take it personally. Conflicted people bring conflict. And even though you have to stand your ground, don't fight back. The Psalmist said, "Seek peace and work to maintain it." A dear elderly lady used to say to me, a young, inexperienced pastor, "Just rise above it." That's not bad advice, regardless of your profession. Within that, remember, maintaining boundaries is essential because some people will dominate you, sucking the joy from your life, draining you of the energy you need for the ones who matter most.

And sometimes people surprise us. In my first full time pastorate, I didn't mow the lawn of the church parsonage. Soon after I had I arrived, one of the church members grumbled to me, "Our former pastor mowed the lawn." I responded, tongue in cheek, "Well, I called him and he doesn't want to come back and mow it." The disgruntled church member wasn't amused with my stab at humor.

Life Matters   *153*

But in time, my grumpity critic invited me to join him and some others on a mission trip to help build a church in Indiana. And I hesitatingly agreed. Maybe it happened on the road trip, or perhaps it was in working side by side, but somewhere in the process, he ceased to be "a lot of work" and became a friend. He requested that I preside at his funeral. And years later, I did.

Sometimes, not often, but sometimes, those "a lot of work" people enlighten our eyes to new and fascinating vistas of life. After all, in that movie, *Sea of Love*, Helen Kruger forgave Frank Keller (Al Pacino), and if they got married, she would have become Helen Keller.

People are work, but sometimes they can help us see that even in darkness, there is light.

It's in your smile--April 4, 2011

I was at one of my favorite restaurants, Jason's Deli, when I noticed the man sitting at another table, eating with his wife and three young children. He was a big, raw-boned, burly guy, who towered over me when I walked by him, both of us on our way to sit down. He plopped onto his chair, perhaps exhausted from work. I slid into the booth with my wife.

That's when I took a good look at him. Stern-faced and serious, he cast what seemed like an intimidating aura over his family as they ate together.

On a second trip to the salad bar, I couldn't help but overhear a piece of his conversation with his oldest boy, who appeared to be about 8 or 9 years old. "You got three RBIs, but I think you can do even better," he said, rather gruffly, obviously referring to his son's little league baseball game.

Immediately I began creating a personality profile of the man. "He must be one of *those* dads," I thought to myself. You know, the father who pushes his children to excel in sports. As he sat there at the dinner table with his brow furrowed, his big hand enveloping his fork, which he used with rapid-fire efficiency to attack his food, and his broad shoulders slightly slumped over his plate, I found myself visualizing him at the ball park, barking orders to his son to throw farther, hit harder, and run faster.

Interesting, isn't it, how quickly we form first impressions, and in our mind create an image of what someone is like? Based on someone's facial expression, body language, demeanor, and dress we make a quick evaluation. And, once our opinion is formed, it's difficult to change it.

Evolutionary psychologists argue that making snap judgments is an evolutionary adaptation necessary for survival: life or death situations demanded speedy decisions. The prehistoric hunter couldn't dally before concluding either to run from a wooly mammoth or gather a team of hunters and spear it for dinner. And assembling a team of hunters was itself an evolutionary social development that required quick evaluations.

In his book, *Blink: The Power of Thinking Without Thinking*, Malcolm Gladwell, concludes, "The only way human beings could ever have survived as a species as long as we have is that we've developed another kind of decision-making apparatus that's capable of making very quick judgments based on very little information."

Inviting a co-worker over for dinner, for example, is a conscious decision. It's something we think through. A spontaneous decision to argue with that co-worker is made unconsciously from a different part of the brain. "Whenever we meet someone for the first time, whenever we interview someone for a job, whenever we react to a new idea, whenever we are faced with making a decision quickly and under stress, we use that second part of the brain," says Gladwell.

Sizing up that dad at Jason's Deli, I was forming an instant image of who he was. And imagining him swaggering over to my table and demanding my dessert, that part of my brain that evaluates danger would instantly process the situation--and estimating the size of his arms compared to mine, his large body frame next to my smaller one, a spontaneous decision would be made: relinquish the dessert, grab my wife, and run to the car.

Then something unexpected happened that totally changed my image of this man.

 The big guy got up with his wife and kids to leave. For some reason, I glanced at his children, and approvingly smiled at them. Then my eyes met his, and in that unspoken communication, one dad connected with another dad, one father--with a daddy-smile to another's children, spoke to the other dad without saying a word, "I see your precious children, and they are beautiful."

In that moment, his stiff upper lip melted into a soft smile, and with his eyes gleaming, it was as if he said, "Thanks, I appreciate that."

My image of the dad was suddenly transformed from that of a hard-driving, performance-requiring, disciplining-demanding sergeant into a teddy-bear of a pappa--a daddy who might invite his kids to sit in his lap while he read *Winnie-the-Pooh*, a guy who could break into a grin, and nodding in agreement to my smile, whisper, "Aren't kids great?"

It happened, all in an instant.

First impressions can't be avoided. But they aren't always right. And when we are willing to take a second or third, longer look--and maybe flash a sincere smile--our whole perception can change for the better.

Pardon my Blush--February 6, 2012

I could feel the veins in my face grow suddenly warm as I imagined my cheeks glowing bright red, signaling to all that I was blushing.

It happened in the post office. Clinking shut the little door to my mail box, I whirled around to see the usual long line waiting at the counter. And there with her back turned to me was one of my parishioners. I sneaked up to her and bending my finger to form a knuckle, tapped her on the arm, mouthing a clicking sound as I did, thinking she would laugh when she saw that it was me, her pastor who was teasing her.

Only when she turned around in surprise, it wasn't my friend; it was a complete stranger.

"Oh, I am so sorry," I attempted an apology as I stepped away from her. "I... I thought you were someone else."

By now, everyone else in line had turned around, curious to see what was happening, wondering what exactly I had done to this innocent victim of my misplaced prank. I thought I noticed one lady edging closer to the counter.

I backed out of the post office, in the words of Roberta Flack, "all flushed with fever."

Later that day, right after lunch, I happened to see my friend's son-in-law downtown. I told him my story of how I had thought I had seen his mother-in-law at the post office but startled someone else. We both laughed.

Moments later, back at the office, I glanced in the mirror.

What was that on the side of my face? Oh my goodness, a splotch of brown balsamic vinaigrette salad dressing from lunch. Now I wondered if the son-in-law was laughing at my story or the brown tobacco-juice-looking stain glaring on the side of my mouth.

And again, I felt, "all flushed with fever."

That evening, I was telling my wife the story of my two faux paus.

"Did you have any appointments this afternoon?" she asked.

"Just one," I answered. "Why?"

"Because you've got mustard on the front of your shirt."

She wasn't kidding--there it was, bright shining and yellow, between the third and fourth buttons.

It was all in a day's work: Through each awkward event, I felt that rush of blood to my cheeks and a faint light-headedness.

It's called blushing, and scientists believe it's is a common human reflex that developed in our evolutionary process over tens of thousands of years. It's akin to a "flight or fight" response to our nervous system, an involuntary reaction. We have a sudden rush of adrenaline, our pupils grow larger, and our digestive system slows down to allow the blood flow to be directed to our muscles.

One theory is that blushing came to signal that a social norm had been broken. Neuroscientist Mark Changizi in his book, *The Vision Revolution* (BenBella, 2009), claims that we developed unusually strong color vision so that we could detect subtle hue changes in other peoples' skin and could thereby deduce their emotions. His results "showed that in the context of transgressions and mishaps, blushing is a helpful bodily signal with face-saving properties. It seems therefore unwise to hide the blush or to try not to blush in these types of contexts."

In other words, blushing actually evokes sympathy and in effect disarms an otherwise threatening situation.

Ahh, so that explains that dear lady's kindness to me in the post office, "That's okay, I understand," I thought I heard her say as she beamed an empathic grin. And what's a little tobacco, I mean balsamic vinaigrette, on the side of the mouth but a cue for more sympathy? And mustard dribbled down the front of my shirt? Bring on the compassion.

Come to think of it, as I reflect on that day, I believe I was the recipient of more warm heartedness than usual.

I'm getting up extra early tomorrow to practice a little blushing. And if I can't come by it that way, I'll just wear a brown penny loafer on my left foot and a black wing tip on my right.

One missing child still too many--May 16, 2012

I know how easy it is for a child to be abducted. That's because when I was a child, I invited a stranger into my home.

It was 1963, I was in second grade, and Mom was at PTA meeting. I had been allowed to come home and stay by myself rather than wait at school until the meeting was over.

That's when the stranger rang the doorbell.

I shouldn't have opened the door, but I did, anyway. I shouldn't have answered his question about where my parents were, telling him I was home alone, but I did, anyway. And I shouldn't have invited him in when he flipped a shiny silver dollar in the air, promising me it would be mine if I would let him in and give him something to eat. I shouldn't have.

But I did, anyway.

And in an instant, I, a child, was alone in my house with a complete stranger.

I suppose there are as many ways to abduct a child as there are children to be abducted. In the US about 800,000 children are reported at least temporarily missing every year, although only about 115 become victims of what is viewed as stranger abductions.

Being vigilant about the potential for child abductions is now woven into our social fabric: We alert our children to "stranger danger;" we know Amber Alert; we try to teach our children how to respond to a potentially dangerous situation; we have a communal fear of a child being taken: We no longer raise our children in an age of innocence.

Much of our safeguard against child abductions is a result of the ones who didn't make it back home. Etan Patz never returned after he was allowed for the first time to walk by himself to the school bus in the quiet, supposedly safe SoHo neighborhood of Manhattan 33 years ago. His became one of the first cases to utilize technology and media to try and find a missing child. Not only were flyers distributed on telephone poles throughout New York City, but Etan's face was on every milk carton in America.

Community awareness and technological advances have been successful. Ernie Allen, president of the National Center for Missing & Exploited Children has noted, "More than 99 percent of children reported missing in America in recent years have come home alive."

Technology has created other possibilities as well. Steve Carter, a 35 year old software salesman, found himself on a missing children's website. Last year, Steve, a resident of Philadelphia, was watching CNN'S coverage of Carlina White, the Atlanta woman who discovered she had been kidnapped from a Harlem hospital in 1987 by a women posing as a nurse. A website for missing children helped clue Carlina into her missing past.

That story made Steve even more curious about his own biological family, so on a hunch, he clicked on missingkids.com. He found an age-progression image of himself as an infant. With the exception of the haircut, the resemblance was remarkable. His biological mom had apparently given him to a Honolulu orphanage, changing Steve's name. Now, he has been reunited with his biological father.

Having eaten the roast beef sandwich I had prepared from Sunday's lunch, the stranger in my house paused as if he were a connoisseur of fine desserts, liking his lips, anticipating an after dinner treat.

I gazed at the floor.

I can still feel his eerie stare like the hot breath on the neck of an animal being pursued by a predator.

Then, as if he sensed my apprehension, he suddenly became a salesman and pulling out a picture album, he opened it and began showing portraits of children, picture after picture of boys and girls. They looked like pictures of children suitable for a church pictorial directory.

But they weren't.

"Would you like to go with me and have your picture made?" he asked. Having my picture made didn't sound the least bit appealing and besides, I told the stranger, my mom would be home any minute, and he could ask her.

"You don't have to ask her," the stranger whispered, and in the next breath, he asked to use the phone.

He made a call to the Weston Hotel, which I later learned carried the seediest of reputations in our town.

I don't recall the details of his short conversation, but he abruptly hung up the phone with declaration and announced, "Sorry, kid, I've got to go."

And he hustled out the door, without a mention of the silver dollar.

Later that afternoon, Mom was interrogating my older brother, Mark, about the mysterious disappearance of the roast beef. That's when I told Mom, matter of factly, what had transpired while she was at PTA.

At once there was a flurry of activity. Dad was suddenly home, the police arrived, I was questioned, and later, late in the night, taken to the police station and asked to pick out the suspect in a line-up.

The stranger wasn't among them.

Who told him to leave my house? And why didn't he take me? Did he move on to abduct other children? And who were those children in the photo album?

The possibilities are as frightening as the ones that could have happened to me.

It's comforting to be a part of the many who were never abducted or among the 99% who were but returned safely home.

It's the 1% that haunts me. For I was most surely almost among them.

Jesus told about leaving the 99 and searching for the lost one: "If a man has a hundred sheep and one of them wanders away, what will he do? Won't he leave the ninety-nine others on the hills and go out to search for the one that is lost?" (Matthew 18:12).

Why does he go? Because the Father cares.

And knows: "I have called you by name; you are mine" (Isaiah 43:1).

Even when their names are changed and their background erased, the Father knows who the missing children are and to whom they belong.

And even when their life is lost, he has found them.

There's a cat in our house!--May 15, 2012

My wife was doubled over, laughing hysterically at me. And I wasn't the least bit amused.
A recent storm had unhinged the door to the crawl space beneath our house. For a few days, our two Schnauzers, Max and Baylor, had been nervously smelling the floor vents. I finally put my ear to one of them and heard it: a faint but unmistakable meow.

A cat was under our house.

My apologies to cat lovers: I am not one of you. Cats and I have an understanding: I don't bother them, and they don't bother me. It's not that I'm actually scared of cats; they just make me nervous. And the closer I get to one, the more uneasy I become. My natural defenses kick in. If your friendly cat jumps in my lap, I will smile, and say, "Nice kitty," but I will be suppressing a flinch; your lovable pet will put me on edge.

So, ok, maybe I am a borderline feline phobiac.

I can trace my cat aversion to my childhood friend's cat. Rex Martin's cat joined us as we were playing under a cardboard table with a sheet over it, pretending it was a secret hide-a-way. All was well until something made his cat want out. I was in the way. Rex was laughing uncontrollably at the specter of his cat wrapped up with me in that sheet, the cat clawing and scratching, me crying and screaming.

The cat did eventually find its way out, but when it was over, a permanent maker had written the words in my memory with large letters: BEWARE OF CATS. In fact, it took a birthday party with cake and ice cream to coax me back over to Rex's house. Even then, I stood on the doorstep and required the promise of cat security before I would enter.

So, the other night, when I realized a cat was underneath our house, I first tried leaving the crawl space door open, hoping the cat would find its way cat out. Nothing doing. Finally, that fateful night, Lori leaned over the vent in our kitchen. "I hear it too," she whispered. "Poor kitty, probably starving."

Then she did the unthinkable. Pulling the grate off the vent she called, "Here kitty." I stepped back, shaking my head, "no," but before I could warn her not to do that again, she did it, "Here kitty, up here kitty."

Then it happened.

Maybe it was Lori's sweet voice, or perhaps it was the smell of dog food to a hungry cat, but it happened.

Suddenly that cat crawled up the vent and into our house. Lori ran to open the door, but the Schnauzers intercepted the cat, chasing the feline fugitive around, under, and over the kitchen table.

Where was I? I don't know how I got there, but I was standing on our couch, horrified, palms of my hands on the side of my head screaming, "There's a cat in our house!"

The cat circled around the couch where I was standing, Max and Baylor in hot pursuit. Lori took one look at this bewildering scene, and like Rex Martin of years ago, howled with laughter.

I was pointing to the grate, thinking one of us should put it back over the vent, forcing the cat out the door. I froze; Lori kept laughing.

And then, as quickly as that cat had emerged from the underworld of my house, it found its way back down, a cat's paw in front of the Schnauzers who screeched to a halt, yapping and peering down the vent at the disappearance of the cat's tail.

Lori was trying to gain her composure; the Schnauzers ran to me, stopped in front of the couch, and looked up as if to say, "That was so much fun, can we do it again?"

And there I was: standing alone on the crouch, feeling like Quasimodo before the crowd, crowned the king of fools.

Some stories have profound moral implications; others are simple reminders that most of us suppress secret, seemingly silly fears deep within our psyche. And sometimes it helps to know that about ourselves. And even admit it. It might make us more understanding of others' anxieties.

In case you're wondering, I, yes even I, finally got the cat out alive from beneath the house and in doing so, somewhat redeemed myself.

But that's another story.

Chapter Ten

Sports Matter

It Breaks Your Heart--June 6, 2010

Angelo Bartlett Giamatti, former President of Yale University and before his untimely death in 1989 at the age of 51, the 7th Commissioner of Major League Baseball, said of the game he loved, "It breaks your heart. It is designed to break your heart."

Anyone who watched the replay of Armando Galarraga's elation in that split second when he rightly assumed he had pitched the perfect baseball game--only the 21st perfect game in baseball history, the first 28-out perfect game, the first perfect game for a Detroit Tiger pitcher--anyone who watched him rise to baseball heaven in that ecstatic moment, anyone who winced in sympathy with his pain when an umpire snatched him from it in an instant, pulling him from the joy, pushing him to the agony, and all because of a botched call, anyone who watched the replay where perfect was called imperfect, flawless declared flawed, faultless found blemished, anyone who watched the wry smile on Galarraga's face at the realization of the loss, anyone who saw the tears of personal disappointment on umpire Jim Joyce's face upon admitting he made an enormously inexcusable mistake, anyone who viewed that historic scene would agree with Giamatti, "It breaks your heart."

And that's why I love baseball.

Baseball is life, really. Not in the sense that it in itself gives us a meaning, a purpose, or a reason for living. Rather, the game of baseball mirrors so many of life's realities: it is completely fair and subject to an umpire's mistake; it's frequently dramatic and often mundane; it's intense and relaxing; it keeps you on the edge of your seat while you wait and wait for something, anything, to happen; it's a game in which many are overpaid and more don't earn enough, a game where a player's mistakes might be published daily and his perfections forgotten in a moment; it is a sport that displays the spoiled rottenness of some and the graceful compassion of others. Just like life.

And that brings me back to pitcher Armando Galarraga and umpire Jim Joyce. Joyce, who is by no means an incompetent, made a mistake. Until he saw the replay, he was convinced had made right call. As soon as he recognized he hadn't, he headed to the Tiger's clubhouse to apologize, requesting to speak personally with Galarraga. Joyce then publicly apologized with sincere sympathy for Galarraga: "I took a perfect game away from that kid over there who worked his (*#*!) off all night." And Galarraga graciously accepted. "He really feels bad, probably more bad than me," he said. In a public display of forgiveness, the next night Gallarraga presented the lineup card to Joyce at the beginning of the game. Both shook hands. Then, Joyce wept.

This baseball episode will be a favorite rerun more for the authentic and spontaneous exhibition of compassion and forgiveness in the leading characters' roles than for the missed call or the perfect game.

And isn't that like life when lived as it should and can be? What we give in love, kindness, and forgiveness is what endures. We often make mistakes, sometimes enormous ones, publicly. And it's embarrassing. But, every now and then we get it all together at just the right moment. It's perfect, beautiful. But it only takes one person who mistakes a work of art for the mediocrity of an amateur, and the hopes, dreams, and aspirations of the artist can die in an instant. And sometimes the artist and judge are one and the same: ourselves. It's then, when we, the judge or the artist, must do what Joyce and Galarraga did: admit our mistake and extend the hand of forgiveness, knowing in our heart that when we pitch the perfect game, no one can take it away, even when no one recognizes it for what it truly is, even when no one recognizes it at all.

And that's life. It breaks your heart. It's designed that way.

The Dream is Bigger than the Game--August 30, 2010

It had taken us three years to accomplish our goal, but we did it, last weekend.

Three years ago my oldest son, Dave, and I talked about our wish list for the baseball parks we wanted to visit. That included some of the oldest and most prestigious stadiums in professional baseball: Fenway in Boston, Yankee Stadium (now the new Yankee Stadium, not the one we dreamed of) in New York City, and Wrigley Field in Chicago. Of course, the new Busch Stadium, home of our favorite team, the St. Louis Cardinals, was a must. Dodger Stadium was high on our list too, as was the Great American Ball Park, home of the Cincinnati Reds.

But time--I do have three other kids, plus Dave and I didn't want to be away for more than a day--and money, we didn't have much, forced us to narrow our list to the ballparks within a day's drive that wouldn't require an overnight stay. That left three ballparks: Bush Stadium (St. Louis), Wrigley Field (Chicago), and the Great American Ball Park (Cincinnati).

We started in Chicago three years ago (Wrigley turned out to be my favorite ballpark, although it doesn't host my favorite team) where we watched the Cubbies defeat our Cards, moved last year to St. Louis where our Redbirds beat the Orioles, and just last weekend we ended up in Cincinnati where we witnessed the Reds pounding of the Cubs.

As we were driving back after the Cincinnati game, we thought of making another run of it, a new three year plan: why not the new Yankee Stadium, the Oriole Park at Camden Yards in Baltimore, and Nationals Park in D.C.? How about an East Coast Baseball Dream? "Yeah," I said, "that would be awesome," even as I was thinking of the time and money, mainly the money.

After leaving Dave at Centre College in Danville, KY., I drove on alone to Lebanon, KY., and deep in my thoughts, wondered what was so important about those games. The atmosphere of the ballpark is great, but it's more than that. You couldn't pay me to go to a ball game and sit by myself. Then I reflected on the movie, *Field of Dreams*, and the words of "Terrence Mann," played by James Earl Jones, who said, in that luxurious voice of his: "People will come Ray. They'll come to Iowa for reasons they can't even fathom... And they'll watch the game and it'll be as if they dipped themselves in magic waters. The memories will be so thick they'll have to brush them away from their faces. People will come, Ray. This field, this game: it's a part of our past, Ray. It reminds of us of all that once was good and it could be again."

I got it. We went to Wrigley, and Busch, and the Great American Ball Park, not to study stadium architecture, but to relive baseball moments of former days: summer evenings at the Astrodome in Houston, TX., a blistering afternoon at the Ball Park in Arlington, TX., many a sweltering practice at the Prien Lake Little League Park in Lake Charles, LA., and our own imaginary games (our team always managed to win) in our front yard everywhere we've lived. And with every ball park we enter, those memories are resurrected; they're embedded in our psyche, drawn forth with the aroma of fresh, roasted peanuts, the echo of the crowd in the stadium's corridors, and the shout of the umpire, "Batter Up!" Ghost ballparks come alive too, like the old Sportsman's Park, grandfather of the new Busch Stadium, where in 1963, I sat enthralled, watching Stan the Man Musial in his last year of play, thinking to myself as I scanned the stadium while chomping down on a hot dog as big as myself, "I'm in a real baseball stadium."

I don't know where we will be next year--maybe we'll revisit one of the ballparks, but wherever we are, I want to be all there, living a dream-- completely alive in that moment.

"Thanks for taking me, Dad, we did it."

"You're welcome, Dave, but we're not done yet. Keep dreaming."

Are you out of your mind? Or is it March Madness?--March 31, 2011

What causes us--normally restrained, responsible people with jobs and families--to lose our minds, whoop and holler, jump up and down, pump our fists in the air, and shout "YES!" as we high five each other?

It's March Madness, of course, the NCAA Division I basketball tournament which results in the national champion. And if your team didn't make it, you can find a favorite. For me, it's usually an underdog--and with the bracket Kentucky had to claw through this year, they surely qualify as one.

In the surprising moments that that make March Madness what it is, anything can happen. For a few hours, we forget about the heavy stuff: economic uncertainties, tragedy in Japan, turmoil in the Middle East, stress at work, problems at home, and we breathe in the moments that make March Madness what it is. In the words of Dick Vitale, "It's unbelievable, baby!"

But wait a minute, before you stay up too late enjoying the Kentucky-UConn matchup this Saturday night, you might want to know there's something amiss on the court, and it's not a conspiracy by the referees to give the Big East representative an advantage over the Cats.

No, it's more serious than even that, according to U.S. Secretary of Education, Arne Duncan. The real March Madness is the fact that 10 of the 68 teams invited to the NCAA tournament this year did not meet the Knight Commission on Intercollegiate Athletics proposal that teams should be eligible for postseason play only if they are graduating at least half of their players. Although Duncan acknowledges that the NCAA has made progress in boosting the academic performance of Division I basketball teams, there is still much, much work to do.

And that's not all: In the last five NCAA tournaments, 44% of the $409 million distributed to the teams with top performances went to teams not on track to graduate at least 50% of their players.

But that's not all. There's more; it gets worse. Not only did 10 of the 68 teams fail to meet the Knight Commissions proposals, but there also exists a growing disparity between the graduation rates of blacks and whites, with a national average of 91% of white players graduating compared with 59% of blacks. (The University of Kentucky graduated 31% of their black players, compared to 100% of their white teammates.)

And March Madness gets more problematic. Richard Vedder and Matthew Denhart, in an article published by *The Wall Street Journal*, contend that this whole business of March Madness is just that, a business, specifically a business in which the athletes are being exploited by the coaches they play for and universities they represent. The athletes bring in much more revenue for the university's athletic program and the bloated salaries of the coaches than the players receive in return. The authors suggest that the players should unionize, or something like that.

And silly me, all I wanted to do was enjoy a March Madness moment. After all, isn't it the moment we wait for? It's the team's go-to-man charging down the court with only a few seconds left, the ball leaving his fingertips, the crowd cringing, the ball swishing through the net just as the buzzer signals game over. One team rejoices in victory; the other falls prostrate on the floor. Isn't that it--the reason we watch, and isn't that why we lose our minds over a game?

I believe it is. It's Kentucky coach John Calipari flashing that proud papa smile at DeAndre Liggins as coach embraces player; it's Virginia Commonwealth coach Shaka Smart leaving the court with the net around his neck; it's Kansas star Markieff Morris crying as he walks slowly off the court. Yes, the moment.

The real March Madness is caught up in a series of moments the summation of which is a collective craziness that helps us keep our sanity for the real world we must face on Monday morning.

So, for a brief period of time this weekend, I'm going to enjoy the moment. I'm going to put the Knight Commission's proposals on the backburner;

I'm not going to think about the graduation ratio and the question of whether players should band together for a better deal than an opportunity for a college education and a chance to make a lot of money.

I'm going to enjoy the moment, and if I run yelling and screaming through the house as the Kentucky Wildcats score the winning basket, don't accuse me of being out of my mind. It's only March Madness.

The Republican Debates Invade College Game Day--October 17, 2011

While awaiting the Republican presidential candidates' debate, I fell asleep, sitting there on my couch. I awoke with a jolt, glanced at my watch, and realized the debates had already started. Hurriedly turning the channel to CNN, I anticipated the debate, this one broadcast live from Las Vegas.

Instead I got College Game Day. I flipped the channel back and tried again: still College Game Day. I checked my clicker and tried once more: College Game Day again. In fact, every channel on TV was College Game Day.

I rubbed my eyes. "This can't be," I thought, "I must be in some kind of media warp."

But there was Chris Fowler hosting College Game Day, "Live," he was saying, "from Las Vegas."

"What?" I asked. "The Republican debate on College Game Day?"

But the camera spanned the football stadium, and sure enough, right there on the field, the Republican presidential candidates were warming up in football uniforms.

Then I saw the Game Day crew: Fowler, Lee Corso, Kirk Herbstreit, and Desmond Howard. It was true; I could hear them speaking:

FOWLER: "This promises to be another wild one."

HERBSTREIT: "No, doubt. And you've got to like Herman Cain as a favorite tonight. He's rocketed like a meteor to the top of the polls and appears to be on a roll; his offense is really clicking with that 9-9-9 plan. It's amazing, but this unlikely candidate could run the tables and find himself in a BCS bowl or even in the Championship Game with President Obama."

CORSO: "Not so fast! Michelle Bachman has slipped, but she's not done yet. The feisty little former IRS tax attorney has an aggressive offense that will shred that 9-9-9 plan by exposing its inconsistencies and mistakes. Cain better be ready! He could go down as quickly as he shot to the top."

HOWARD: "I don't think any of you guys comprehend the efficiency and professionalism of Mitt Romney's offense and defense. He may not be very exciting, but he's paid his dues and has the experience to get the job done. And just look at him down there warming up. That uniform fits him perfectly. I mean, he looks sooo quarterbackish."

HERBSTREIT: "Well, I tell you, Obama would love to face off with him; the clash between Obamacare and Romneycare could be revealing, an epic matchup."

CORSO: "Not so fast, again! You're forgetting Governor Perry. Remember, you don't mess with Texas."

FOWLER: "Where is the governor, anyway? I haven't seen him on the field."

HOWARD: "He's just reentered the stadium. He was scheduled to appear at a pre-game prayer breakfast, and now he seems to be scooting away from a preacher who's wearing a T-shirt that says, 'Thank God I'm a Baptist,' on one side and 'Mormons Need not Apply,' on the other."

At that moment, President Obama himself joined the Game Day crew, smiling, wearing sun glasses, and sporting a ball cap that said, "It's not my Fault." (41% of the fans booed; 22% cheered; and 37% were chanting, "We want Chris Christie.")

FOWLER: "Welcome, Mr. President. Hey, how much did you pay for that snazzy cap?"

PRESIDENT OBAMA: "$29.25, including tax."

CORSO: "Taxes, ugh. That's ridiculously high!"

PRESIDENT OBAMA: "You've got to remember the financial situation I inherited from my predecessor and what with this Republican Congress…"

CORSO: "Oh, I wasn't being critical; I think you're doing a fine job."

PRESIDENT OBAMA: "You do? Really? Oh, well, sorry, in that case, I'll just sit down and scout these candidates as they rip each other. And, haha, I don't even have to get sweaty and dirty! I can just relax and enjoy the show."

Everyone laughed; the College Game Day crew faded as the camera spanned the lights of Vegas from far above the city.

Then I thought I could hear someone call out my name: "David, David."

It was my wife: "You must have fallen asleep again," she consoled.

"You won't believe it." I said. "I went to a political debate and a football game broke out. Was it in a dream? Was it just a dream? I know, yes I know. It seemed so very real, seemed so real to me. You may say I'm a dreamer, but I'm not the only one…"

"Sure," she sarcastically quipped.

"She's right," I admitted, "that was just a dream."

Walking away from the TV, I could barely hear David Gregory hosting Meet the Press. "Welcome to today's program," I faintly heard him saying, "our panel of political experts will continue our debate of which college football team will win the national championship…"

Keep the light on: Don't miss the victory--November 3, 2011

I couldn't take it any longer. Fatigued at the end of the work week and convinced my St. Louis Cardinals would not survive Game 6 of the World Series, I turned the light off and was fast asleep by 11:15 p.m., EST.

Early the next morning, Lori asked me who won. "Oh, the Texas Rangers did," I mournfully informed her. "I stayed with the Cardinals until they left the bases loaded and fell behind 7-4."

I didn't go into detail because she is not a baseball fan, but the Cardinals weren't playing well, I thought. Not only had they left the bases loaded and blown a chance to take the lead, they had also committed three errors-- something they hadn't done in a World Series since game 3 of the 1943 Series. I had tried to help my team by repeating my baseball mantra, "Get a hit, get a hit, get a hit, get a hit," or "Strike out, strike out, strike out, strike out," but the baseball gods weren't listening: Our pitchers were getting hammered and even Albert Pujols was hitless. So assured was I that the Cardinals were dead that I had not even bothered to turn on the TV and check the score, just in case...

Just in case of what? That they would win? No way.

I was pouring myself another cup of coffee when I heard Lori shout from upstairs: "David, your team won! They made a comeback and beat the Rangers." I raced to the TV and incredulously watched the 6 a.m. sports summary of the Cardinals' victory; I couldn't believe it, but it happened: They had miraculously won.

I had missed one the greatest World Series games ever.

There was a lot of baseball left after I had called it quits. The Cardinals rallied behind the bats of Pujols, Lance Berkman, and Allan Craig, as the game went back and forth and into extra innings. Twice the Rangers were one strike away from winning the game and the Series. (The last time a team blew a lead with only 1 strike away from the championship was the 1992 Blue Jays in Atlanta.) Then Cardinals David Freese, who would be named the World Series MVP the next night when the Cards won the Series with a 6-2 win over the Rangers, homered in the bottom of the 11th to force the first game 7 of the Series since 2002.

It was described as "one of the best (World Series) games ever," by sports columnist Jeff Passan.

And I missed it.

Later that morning as I was smiling at the thought of their victory, and a bit remorseful at not having cheered them through it, I think I had a tiny inkling of what the followers of Jesus must have felt three days later, after they had turned off the light of hope and cried themselves to sleep, convinced that the stone covering the tomb was a permanent fixture, wondering why they had spent three years following someone who wasn't the Victor after all.

They missed it too.

"You had to be here to believe it," Cardinals manager Tony La Russa said. "We never quit trying. I know that's kind of corny, but the fact is we never quit trying."

And said Cardinals general manager John Mozeliak, "Those two [game-saving] at-bats were epic and historic as far as Cardinal lore. No matter what, if we're down to our last strike, we don't quit."

I understand gentlemen; I'll keep swinging, too.

And most of all, I'll keep the light on and one eye open until He returns in victory.

I won't miss that one.

Life Matters

It's all in the numbers--January 13, 2012

"Why can't you do something like that?" My friend jokingly posed that question to me while we were waiting for a church deacons meeting to begin.

Several of us had been talking about Denver Broncos quarterback Tim Tebow throwing for exactly 316 yards in the Broncos' overtime playoff win over the Pittsburg Steelers. Not only was it a career high for Tebow, it apparently stupefied many because of the apparent correlation of the number 316 to John 3:16, the biblical reference Tebow used to etch on his "eye black," to avoid sun glare, during his days as QB for the Florida Gators.

The Bible verse, Tebow's favorite, says, "For God loved the world so much that he gave his one and only Son, so that everyone who believes in him will not perish but have eternal life." Tebow, easily America's most popular Christian athlete, has had a close public association with that verse.

The 316 total passing yards was not the only 3:16 connection. He also threw for 31.6 yards per completion. And there's more: during the final quarter of the game, the TV rating was 31.6. And one final association with the John reference: Tebow works for two men, both of whom have the first name, John.

Can you hear the background music from the Twilight Zone?

Then again, for more rational thinkers--maybe not.

In answer to the question, "Why can't you do something like that?" I rejoined, "Tim Tebow only had to look at the Pittsburg Steelers' defense, not a bunch of ornery Baptist deacons." (They really can be ornery, but I didn't say that.)

In all seriousness--since some people do take these numbers seriously, maintaining that the statistics point to John 3:16 as a divine affirmation of Tebow's witness--what do we make of this?

I've long believed God uses a variety of ways to draw attention to his Good News. And if the statistics can be used as an opportunity for that discussion, then believers can use it in a positive way.

But they should also be extremely cautious when it comes to reading messages from God into football statistics. As Josh Tinley (*Kneeling in the End Zone: Spiritual Lessons From the World of Sports*) observed in his blog, two of the numbers cited in that playoff game were 31.6, not 3.16.

Why not look for a book in the Bible that has a 31:6, like II Chronicles 31:6, which says in part, "The people... brought in (their) tithes." And, besides, many Bible passages other than John have a 3:16. How do we know that those statistics don't refer to one of them?

Then there is the matter of other football players, who like Tebow, are Christians. For example, Colt McCoy, QB for the Cleveland Browns, is active in the Fellowship of Christian Athletes. Why not see if any of his statistics connect with a Bible passage he has publicly quoted at some time? What would that reveal?

Or, what if an athlete was of another faith, say Islam? Would evangelicals be disturbed if some of his statistics connected with a passage from the Koran?

The point is, we can substantiate all kinds of beliefs--some true, some erroneous--when we gaze long enough in the tea leaves. Michael Shermer, a religious skeptic, uses this truth to challenge the very essence of religion. In his book, *The Believing Brain*, he maintains that the brain is "a belief engine," which looks for and finds confirmation for beliefs in patterns; we naturally find meaning in connecting the dots, infusing those patterns with meaning, which only serves to reinforce the beliefs with which we began.

So, perhaps believers would do better to practice "tebowing" (so named after the way Tebow kneels in prayer on the sidelines) and remember the words he often speaks, "First and foremost, I just want to thank my Lord and Savior, Jesus Christ. He's done so much in my life."

Having done that, leave the statistics to the people in the press box. After all, those stats are only numbers.

And, so much of athletic success--and, yes, even some so-called miracles--is all in the numbers.

Chapter Eleven

The News Matters

Political Ads Gone Wild--October 25, 2010

Mama always said, "Not all attention is good."

Whew, we've seen the truism of mama's dictum in political ads this campaign year. Politicians, Republican and Democrat, conservative and liberal, have in an effort to draw attention to the flaws of their opponents, used attack ads, and more often than not, drawn negative attention to themselves.

Take, for example, "The Ad," in what is now being described as the ugliest campaign in the country, the campaign for the Kentucky U.S. Senate race between Kentucky Attorney General Jack Conway and Dr. Rand Paul. Conway's ad draws attention to Rand Paul's involvement in a secret society while an undergraduate at Baylor University. I do recall as an undergraduate at Baylor in the late 1970s, the group to which Paul would later belong. Known for their pranks and satirical writing, they were not taken seriously; they did not take themselves seriously. "What will they do next?" we would ask. Unfortunately for them, Baylor President Abner McCall did take them seriously, especially when some of them streaked across campus, a popular activity back then. McCall booted them and their running attire or lack thereof, off campus.

Now, Conway has used Paul's involvement in that organization not, presumably, to attack Paul's religion, but to expose him as part of a lunatic fringe, unfit for office. But in the process, everyone gets hurt, not just those involved in this particular political race.

Indeed the ad got attention on all the major television networks and landed Conway interviews with Matt Lauer (NBC Morning Show) and MSNBC's "Hardball," with Chris Mathews. Speaking of the ad, Mathews said, "I think it questions his faith." And Lauer cited Jonathan Chait's statement in the New Republic--which Lauer characterized as a "fairly liberal publication,"--that "This (Conway's ad) is the ugliest, most illiberal political ad of the year."

"That's not exactly an award you want to win," Lauer quipped.

The tragedy of negative ads, of which Conway's is only the latest example, is that it brings everyone down: I wince every time I see the commercial, "Did Paul really do that?" Then I wince even more, "Did Conway really run that ad?" Stuart Rothenberg correctly dubbed the ad a "thermonuclear bomb."

It hurts not only both candidates, but all of us, although Conway may not realize that yet. Supposing it does work, and he pulls it off, what does it say about the emerging trend in the political process?

It says to anyone with future political aspirations: "If you've ever, done anything inappropriate or perhaps even borderline inappropriate, it can and will be used against you." The danger here is that we will lose qualified, effective leaders who could help America revive from a punishing recession, change the bleak economic forecast, compete with countries and their growing economies, and more effectively face the unknown challenges beyond the current horizon. We lose potential leaders' wisdom; we lose their acumen; we lose their abilities. We all lose. Why? Because we have allowed an environment to thrive that few wish to enter. After all, who wants to put themselves or their families through political hazing? Columnist Peggy Noonan, no newcomer to American politics, recently wrote in her *Wall Street Journal* column about speaking with an entrepreneur, an effective leader with fresh ideas that could help our country. When Noonan urged him to enter politics, his response was, "I've lived an imperfect life. They'd kill me." And they would.

Attack ads have another devastating effect: They spawn cynicism, fuel frustration, and create skepticism among the electorate. People are angry with politicians whom they no longer trust and find increasingly harder to believe. In an interview on Fox News, democratic strategist Richard Socarides defended Conway's ad: "When the stakes are high you have to use extreme measures." Who, then, defines, "extreme measures"? Each politician? Having wallowed into the gutter of politics, it's difficult to shake its stench. And politicians seem surprised with an aggravated electorate.

Conway is by no means the only politician to use "extreme measures." His ad simply happens to have the attention at the moment. And that's the problem: Just as water flows naturally to the lowest level, so do we, unless we determine to seek higher ground. And unless we do, the political process will only get sleazier and slimier, as it slips and slides in its descent into chaos. In so doing, we all suffer; it injures all of us. And then, as we look askance at the mayhem in the political arena, which to a large degree determines our national future, we will perhaps with a tinge of sadness be reminded of that other parental warning: "Mama told me not to come."

Those Incredible Doggie Heroes--May 9, 2011

I could have sworn my dog, Max, quietly napping on my left side, perked up when Diane Sawyer introduced the story about the Navy SEAL dogs on the evening news. Max's brother, Baylor, with eyes half closed, was perched like a cat on the arm of the couch. But when Diane mentioned those heroic dogs, he snapped to attention, instantly turning his head in the direction of the television.

At least I thought he did.

My miniature Schnauzers are about as close to being Navy SEAL dogs as I am to being a Navy SEAL myself. But we three enjoyed the story anyway.

Those Navy SEAL dogs are really something. When the 79 valiant Navy SEALS made their surprise visit to the Bin Laden residence, they were accompanied by one of their highly trained canine comrades. These dogs are capable of sniffing out explosives, finding enemies and when necessary, chasing them down. They are highly outfitted too. The dogs wear protective body armor, and some are trained to communicate with their handler up to 1,000 yards away by means a speaker attached to a vest. The vests are equipped with infrared and night vision cameras that allow the handlers to see what the dog sees. The canine commandos are capable of parachuting, rappelling, and swimming. And they can pack more than a punch with a bite that has a force of between 400 and 700 pounds.

Navy SEAL dogs are not the only doggie heroes. Dogs can be trained not only to detect bombs but to sniff out cancer as well. According to Japanese research published online by the *British Medical Journal*, studies have confirmed that a cancer scent exists and may be circulating in the body. Dogs are capable of nosing out cancer in stool and breath samples.

According to a report on ABC news, Dr. Sheryl Gabram-Mendola, a breast surgical oncologist at Winship Cancer Institute of Emory University, maintains that cancer causes the body to release certain organic compounds that dogs can smell but people cannot. She and her team of researchers developed a test that allows dogs to smell the breath for evidence of cancer in the body.

"Dogs smell different things and they understand different things," says Charlene Bayer, a principal research scientist at Georgia Tech Research Institute. "They may not know what's wrong, but they know there's something that's not normal, that you don't smell the way you normally do," she told ABC news.

As Diane Sawyer closed the evening news report on the Navy SEAL dogs, I was feeling better and better about my own furry companions' distant relationship with those doggie heroes. Neither one of my Schnauzers can ferret out terrorists or corner criminals. The only thing Baylor is trained to do is roll over on his back so I can dry his wet paws, and Max, faithful dog that he is, doesn't even do that, although when I command him to quit digging in the dirt, he obeys almost 50% of the time. But, perhaps like their cancer detecting counterparts who can sense when something's wrong with us physically, they do curl up to any family member who isn't feeling well, and they will bark furiously when a stranger, or a bird for that matter, enters our property. And what would my morning be without the dogs begging me for a hug?

As I clicked the channel to another station, both dogs simultaneously raised their noses as if to sniff something. Were they about to detect an explosive in the room? Were they going to smell a terrorist hiding in the house?

Nope. Instead of sniffing, they yawned, closed their eyes, and silently slipped back to sleep.

The Rapture Racket: Cashing in on the Apocalypse--May 25, 2011

Oops. He missed it again--the date for the rapture, that is. But that's okay, miscalculating the date for the end times is nothing new for Harold Camping.

In 1992 he published his book, *1994?* in which he predicted September 6, 1994 as the beginning of the end. Undeterred by that non-happening, Camping did some re-calculating and published another book in 2008, *We Are Almost There!* He conveniently forgot to mention his 1994 prediction's failure to launch.

Then, last summer, Camping and his followers made another effort to spread the word: "The rapture is nigh!" Specifically, May 21, 2011. At exactly 6 p.m.

Now that it didn't happen, I suppose Camping will anticipate another date. That's what one of his followers, Robert Fitzpatrick--who plunked his entire life savings of $140,000 into advertising the rapture--is doing.

Give it some time, and we can anticipate more of the same from rapture rousers.

That's because there is something comforting in being assured that you will escape the worst of times by being whisked into the heavenlies. And the harder the times, the more urgent becomes the call for the apocalypse.

People are curious; they want to know: when will it happen?

Those who claim to know created a rapture racket that has reaped big financial dividends.

According to Family Radio's IRS filings, contributions and grants to Camping's organization topped $18 million last year. Warning the doomed of their fate in the predicted apocalypse wasn't cheap. Family Radio spent as much as $1 million on the billboard campaign alone. But, what's a mere $1 million when your radio network's net worth is about $122 million?

So, when 6 p.m. May 21, 2011 came and passed uneventfully, Harold Camping may have been hurt, but not financially. He still sat on a personal net worth estimated at $72 million.

That's right, $72 million.

"$72 million," I whimsically thought to myself at approximately 6:01 p.m. Saturday as I scanned the horizon for any paranormal activity. Later, I repeated the figure aloud to myself, sitting in my lawn chair on our back patio, picturing how many hungry and homeless people could be fed and housed with just half of $72 million, and fantasizing what I would do with just a fraction of the revenue gleaned from the rapture racket.

Camping is not the only one who has profited from the prediction of the world's end. Bart Centre, an atheist, sells insurance policies to those who might be worried about what will happen to their pets in the event that the raptured believers will leave their dearly beloved behind.

Then there is Mark Herrod, who according to the *Wall Street Journal* is a 52-year-old Evangelical Christian who created a business for believers wanting emails sent to friends and relatives in the event of the rapture. He has over 100 clients who pay $14.95 a month for the service.

And then there are those who hawked T-Shirts and assorted paraphernalia. There was the "I Survived Judgment Day! and All I Got Is This Lousy T-Shirt" shirt for $25, the "2011 Rapture Survivor" mug ($15), the "Darn, I Slept Through Judgment Day" baby onesie ($15), and the truism, "If you can read this, we're both sinners--5-21-11," available in shirt, mug or thong ($15-25).

And I'm on the patio, warmed by the glow of the setting sun even as I'm plagued by thoughts of the homeless, hungry and hurting, and yes, rising expenses in my own house.

Then, I recall that Jesus never promised it would be easy this side of eternity, even though ultimate victory is promised to the believer. The trouble is, we just don't know what the date is for that final triumph, for Jesus himself put a damper on rapture predicting when he said, "No one knows the day or hour when these things will happen, not even the angels in heaven or the Son himself" (Matthew 24:36).

And Jesus had stern words for those who focus on the irrelevant as they grab more and more while ignoring the needs of people in front of them: "When you refused to help the least of these my brothers and sisters, you were refusing to help me" (Matthew 25:45).

Now, that's the message I'd like to see on a T-shirt or billboard--somewhere, anywhere. The only problem is--this side of the apocalypse, who on earth will buy it?

Unplug the Drug--May 26, 2011

Why did the news that the Osama bin Laden's residence contained a sizable amount of pornography grab our attention? After all, our culture is saturated with pornography; it's everywhere; it's even an accepted part of life for much of society.

So why are we surprised? Bin Laden--mass murderer that he was--nonetheless exuded an image of religiosity. Professor Akbar Ahmed, Ibn

Khaldun Chair of Islamic Studies at the American University in Washington DC, observed in an interview on ABC news that "it is surprising that pornography was found because he (bin Laden) was known to be a rather austere man, a rather religious man, a man who... gave up the world."

Even if he turned his back on the world, pornography followed bin Laden--at least into his compound. ABC news correspondent Martha Raddatz reported that although we can't know for certain that bin Laden actually viewed the pornography, it was found right there in his bedroom, and according to Reuters news, it was a fairly extensive amount of pornography at that.

It is the suspicion of hypocrisy that attracts our attention. Bin Laden was unequivocal in his denunciation of what he believed was the US exploitation of women. In a 2002 letter to the American people, he railed, "Your nation exploits women like consumer products or advertising tools, calling upon customers to purchase them," he wrote. "You plaster your naked daughters across billboards in order to sell a product without any shame. You have brainwashed your daughters into believing they are liberated by wearing revealing clothes, yet in reality all they have liberated is your sexual desire."

That's a fairly accurate description of a pornographic industry that is worldwide today, an industry that may have seduced an otherwise religious and austere Osama bin Laden.

That's why pornography is usually a private affair: secrecy conceals shame and shuns embarrassment. But hidden habits lend themselves to hypocrisy. And we flinch at hypocrisy, especially when we sense it in a person who wears a religious image.

It's difficult to keep something as potentially powerful as pornography under the bed forever. Like a drug, pornography can be addictive. Scientists surmise that dopamine and oxytocin are released in the male brain during intimacy. According to behavior therapist, Andrea Kuszewski, it's a "biochemical love potion." But, these same neurotransmitters fire when watching porn. "You're bonding with it," says Kuszewski, "and those chemicals make you want to keep coming back to have that feeling." Men, in effect, can develop a neurological attachment to porn.

Of course, the negative downside of that sensual high is that pornography replaces real relationships. In her article, "The Porn Myth," feminist Naomi Wolf argues that the internet has "pornographized," our culture. The effect is that instead of amplifying men's sexual activity with their actual partners, it renders men less sexually responsive to real women. That's because erotic images replace real people.

The result: Some men prefer porn over real life partners. The recently released movie, *No Strings Attached*, has Alvin (Kevin Kline) complaining to his roommate, Adam (Ashton Kutcher), "I can't focus on my porn with all this real sex going on."

With porn on the brain, meaningful intimacy is a challenge. As a 43 year old composer put it an interview with *New York Magazine*: "I've got to resort to playing scenes in my head that I've seen while viewing porn. Something is lost there. I'm no longer with my wife; I'm inside my own head."

No doubt, porn messes with the mind. But it's a matter of the heart as well, as Proverbs 4:23 would remind us: "Above all else guard your heart for it determines the direction of your life." And Jesus of Nazareth took dead aim at those who pretend that as long as it's a secret, it's not really a sin: "Anyone who even looks at a woman with lust has already committed adultery with her in his heart" (Matthew 5:28).

Maybe bin Laden would have agreed with Jesus, since his own holy book, the Qur'an states, "Tell the believing men to lower their gaze and protect their private parts. That is purer for them. Verily, Allah is all-aware of what they do..." (24.30-31)

But apparently it was difficult for bin Laden to unplug the drug of pornography, especially since it was in the privacy of his bedroom, where certainly no one would ever intrude without an invitation.

Should Christians Pray for the Death of President Obama?--January 30, 2012

Although the Republicans have been going at it for several months, we are not yet into the heat of the presidential race, and already some Christians are praying for the early demise of President Obama.

When I say, "demise," I mean death.

At least that's the implication of the recent email sent by Mike O'Neal, the Republican speaker of the Kansas House of Representatives. That email followed a previous one in which O' Neal had referred to Michelle Obama as "Mrs. Yomama."

I doubt O'Neal will be a dinner guest at White House any time soon.

O'Neal is not the first to invoke a prayer for the early exit of President Obama. Soon after his election, some conservative Christians circulated a bumper sticker which called on Christians to pray, tongue-in-cheek, for the president: The "prayer" cites Psalm 109:8, a Bible verse in the form of a "prayer for Obama," which says, "May his days be few; may another take his office."

O'Neal's email was an extension of that bumper sticker mentality.

The problem is in the phrase, which neither O'Neal nor the bumper sticker purveyors quote directly, but which immediately follows their scriptural citation. It reads: "May his children become fatherless, and his wife a widow. May his children wander as beggars and be driven from their ruined homes."

Although O'Neal issued an apology saying he only meant that Obama's days in office be few, the Scripture, taken in context (and O'Neal is apparently interested in the context for his email stated, "At last — I can honestly voice a Biblical prayer for our president! Look it up — it is word for word! Let us all bow our heads and pray. Brothers and Sisters, can I get an AMEN? AMEN!!!!!!") calls not just for the cessation of employment, in this case the presidency, but for the cessation of life for the person of interest, the enemy--in this case President Obama.

For centuries thoughtful Christians have struggled with this passage, since Christians are not supposed to curse their enemies. The psalm is part of a group of psalms called "imprecatory psalms," because they call on God to deal with enemies, in some cases, as in Psalm 109, by removing them from planet Earth. Many of the Early Church Fathers dealt with the problem by interpreting this psalm as a prophesy of Judas, since Peter quoted it in the upper room after the suicide of Jesus' traitor.

Christian apologist and philosopher, C.S. Lewis, spoke of how Psalm 109 "strikes us in the face... like the heat from a furnace mouth." Lewis pointed to the spirit of hatred expressed in these psalms as a way of reminding us of the evil that resides within each of us, directing us to the humility and love we find in the grace and mercy of Jesus Christ.

Certainly Christians should be mindful that Christ's love prevails over hatred and evil. But, in regard to the Scripture O'Neil and other Christians like to cite in hopes of a convenient termination of the Obama administration, they should be mindful that the interpretation of this psalm hinges around verse 6, where the cursing of the enemy begins. Some maintain that David, traditionally believed to be the author of the psalm, is not cursing anyone but is rather quoting those who are cursing him. Indeed, some modern translations, like the New Living Translation, supply the words, "They say," at the beginning of verse six.

In that case, by citing this passage, O'Neal and certain right-wing Christians are actually siding with the enemies of King David, the ones who made the false accusations against God's anointed one, the ones David cried to God for help and protection against, the ones who prompted David to pray: "Let them curse me if they like, but you (God) will bless me!" (Psalm 109:28)

By analogy to the current situation, Obama would be the one falsely accused by the enemies of God--in this case, the Christian right.

Those summoning God to respond to their "Obama prayer" of Psalm 109 should not only reflect on the legitimization of calling on a loving, forgiving, merciful God to slay another Christian (President Obama is a professing Christian, regardless of what one thinks of his political agenda), but they should also be mindful, as they so cavalierly quote Scripture, of whose side they find themselves on.

Praying for the judgment of an enemy is easy.

But loving one is Christian.

And thoroughly biblical.

Why Bad Boys are Bad--April 18, 2012

Last week was a bad week for bad boys.

First, 51 year old Bobby Petrino, at the height of his career, got himself fired as the University of Arkansas football coach for allegedly trying to deceive the University's Athletic Director about the coach's relationship with the 25 year old football employee and former volleyball player, Jessica Dorrell.

Then 11 Secret Service agents were placed on administrative leave for allegedly being involved with prostitutes in Cartagena, Columbia, while preparing for President Obama's visit.

Petrino, the father of four, was one of the top coaches in college football. It took years of successful steps before he could stand in that exclusive realm.

And those secret service agents worked long and hard to gain their honored positions in the Secret Service, an elite group whose job it is to protect the president and other high ranking officials.

Now, the University of Arkansas is embarrassed by Petrino's actions, just as the Secret Service is by those agents.

Why would these men take such a risk?

There's a scene in the movie, *The Help*, where concerned friends are trying to set up Skeeter Phelan (Emma Stone) with a man. The two are making conversation at a restaurant, waiting for their double-date partners to arrive, and already, Skeeter's date is half-drunk and making rude comments. Skeeter, the unsouthern southern girl, wastes no time in telling him what she thinks about him. As she stands up to walk away, she asks, "I'm sorry, but were you dropped on your head as an infant?"

Maybe someone should ask Petrino and the Secret Service agents the same question.

More pointedly, why do men do such incredibly stupid things? After all, Petrino and the 11 men in the Secret Service are only the last in a long line of men who have done stupid things: Tiger Woods, Rick Pitino, Arnold Schwarzenegger, and John Edwards are only a starter list for a huge catalog of names that stretches across history.

It can be traced all the way back to the original stupid guy: Adam.

From the time Adam took the forbidden fruit from Eve, men have been trying to please women.

The problem is, men seem to get confused about which woman to please. Thus, tempted by the fruit of another, men mistakenly imagine the new fruit is different and therefore better than what they already have.

And one bad decision leads to another.

But, where Adam started it, Jesus stopped it, or at least he gave us reason to hope we could. And he understood that we've all done things we've later regretted.

He stood up for one who was about to be stoned to death for getting involved in one of those stupid things. Two people were caught in the very act of adultery; it was only the woman who was dragged before the moral majority. That's when Jesus intervened: "Let the one who has never sinned throw the first stone" (John 8:7).

One by one those arrogant men lowered their heads, dropped their stones, and walked away.

The only one without sin that day turned to the woman and refused to condemn her. Then he left her with a command: "Go and sin no more," he admonished.

That's the seemingly impossible challenge: Stop doing stupid things.

But, he who issued the command gives us himself, and in him, we discover the possibility of fulfilling it.

That should give hope to all of us: bad boys and bad girls.

Pick it up and read it! — June 27, 2012

No, I don't mean the Bible, although I read it every day.

But for now, I'm referring to the newspaper.

"Ahh, the newspaper," you say. "You mean that old dinosaur of the printed era that's somehow managed to stay alive, despite its shrinking advertising revenue and a dwindling subscriber base?"

Despite rumors of its demise, the newspaper is surviving and in some instances, thriving.

I know that's the exception and not the norm. According to a 2010 Harris Poll, 1 in 10 American adults say they never read a daily newspaper, and only 2 of 5 read a daily newspaper, either online or in print.

That's really not surprising, since Americans read less today. According to a 2007 study by the National Endowment of the Humanities, reading levels among young adults has plummeted over the last two decades. The average person between ages 15 and 24 spends 2 to 2 1/2 hours a day watching TV and 7 minutes reading.

So, I was shocked but probably shouldn't have been when I read that *The Times- Picayune*, the paper of New Orleans, La., established in 1837 and winner of several Pulitzer Prizes, will scale down its print edition to three days a week this fall, as will several other newspapers owned by its parent company.

Newspapers have long been a part of my life. Many times, after a day in elementary school, I would wait on my front porch for the afternoon delivery of the *Altus Times-Democrat*. We subscribed to several newspapers. Back then, the *Daily Oklahoman* had a morning edition as well as an evening edition, *The Oklahoma City Times*. I devoured both, as well as the morning edition of *The Lawton Constitution*. Occasionally, Dad would purchase the *Times Record News* of Wichita Falls, TX, but I looked with skepticism upon anything from the Longhorn State.

Sunday afternoon, having feasted on Mom's delicious pot roast, was given to reading the newspaper. My brothers and father would divide out the sections of the paper, and soon they would be strewn about the den, one section on the couch, another across the recliner, each waiting to be read by one of us.

Today, I subscribe to several newspapers and whenever I'm visiting another town or city, I make sure to get a local paper, for each has its unique features reflective of its constituency.

Newspapers keep me aware of the world in which I happen to live.

As blogger Tracey Dickerson has noted, it was the great Swiss theologian, Karl Barth, who in an interview with Time Magazine in 1966, advised young theologians "to take your Bible and take your newspaper, and read both. But interpret newspapers from your Bible."

Barth was reminding believers that although they are not to be of the world, they are yet in it, and as such, they should know the world in which they live. Moreover, Christians should be a discerning, reflective people.

But believers certainly haven't cornered the market on thinking. Whether you think like a theologian or are simply a thinker, the newspaper can stimulate your mind to a broader awareness of what's going on in the world around you, whether it's news about the local community, municipal government, available jobs, the nation, or broader geo-political issues that affect us all, often unknowingly.

Of course, when Barth spoke those words, the internet didn't exist, nor did CNN or Fox News. We have access to news 24/7, through dozens of portals, more news than we can digest.

It shouldn't be a question of either/or but an affirmation of both the internet and the printed page.

The question we must ask ourselves is, what's the quality of the news reports we are getting? Are we receiving information based on thorough investigative reporting?

It's easy to watch any number of news talk shows. I do on occasion. While interesting, and often hosted by knowledgeable and talented people, they are usually, by the very nature of the ratings race, skewed toward drama, hype, and superficiality.

The challenge for newspapers is to provide the financial resources for quality reporting, whether it's reporting by a local or regional paper or one of the major dailies.

How then can newspapers survive? Billionaire Warren Buffett, who is in the process of purchasing 26 daily newspapers and has had success with others, writes that newspapers fail when one more of the following factors are present: (1) the town or city has more than one competing dailies, (2), the newspaper is no longer the primary source of information for the readers, (3) or the town or city does not have a "pervasive identity."

Surviving and even thriving is a challenge, but it's worth the try, and that brings me back to Karl Barth. I've got my Bible in one hand: I've read where it will last forever. It's the newspaper which concerns me, for without it, my application of the Bible to the world would be diminished.

Chapter Twelve

Becoming Your Better Self Matters

The Bully in You--November 1, 2010

It seems bullying is epidemic these days. The cruel facts reveal that 23% of elementary students report being bullied one to three times in the last month; 77% of students report having been bullied; and each day 160,000 kids stay home from school for fear of being bullied.

I remember being bullied. It happened in my own front yard. I was in third grade, maybe fourth. We were playing football when some kids in junior high invited themselves to our game. Being bigger than us, they quickly took the game away. Then it got ugly. They began to call us names, "Punks," "Wimps," "Sissy's." Abusive language for the 1960s. The name calling escalated into pushing and shoving. We were intimidated by these older, bigger kids.

And then, from nowhere, or so it seemed, my older brother, Mark, showed up. Somehow he had seen what was happening. Mark was a stand-out football player for the Altus High School Bulldogs. He walked into our humiliating situation, took the football in his grip and zinged it at one of the bullies. It stung the kid, slipping through his hands and bouncing off his chest. "What's wrong? Can't take a ball thrown that fast?" Mark challenged. "Well, if you can't play with the big boys, why are you picking on these little kids who are younger and smaller than you?"

That's all it took. They lowered their heads and sulked away. Mark tossed the ball back to us and left without saying another word. Nothing more needed to be said. Case closed.

But what happens when no older brother or friend or parent shows up? What happens when our protectors are no longer there? Therein is the problem.

Experts tell us to communicate with others if we are bullied. Tell a parent or some authority. Also, stay in a group, and if possible, stand up to the bully, but don't fight back.

People bully for many reasons. In one survey, 1 in 5 students admitted to having been a bully or bullying others at some point. Perhaps the root cause for bullying is a sense of insecurity which is expressed in a feeling of superiority over someone whose character the bully despises. Unfortunately, gayness has been an object for bullying. In the month of September, 2010, alone, nine young people, gay or suspected of being gay, took their lives after being bullied.

So, what's the solution? Maybe the best place to start is for everyone to take a look within and ask, "Is there a bully in me?"

All of us have voices from the present and past that haunt us and cause us to engage in less than admirable behaviors. Sometimes the bully within whispers in our ear, "You're a loser; you're not worth it; you can't." And so, in frustration, we speak words of condemnation to the child in our home, or our spouse, or that different girl or guy at work or school. And we think somehow the negative feelings we receive from the bully within us will be abated by putting another down. Hurting others will make us feel better, we think. But it's an illusion. It only reinforces negativity; we become less authentically human as a result.

Perhaps the key is to address that bully within. To say, "I am better than that," is not to exalt oneself above others but to acknowledge God's positive plan for us. We can live with others who are different--with red and yellow, black and white, gay and straight, for they are precious in his sight. God loves people. Period. To bully one of God's creatures is an affront to the God who made them. We don't have to bully others to prove who we are. We just have to embrace the "Yes," from the One who loves us always, just as we are, so we can love others just like they are. And then enjoy a life lived with that forever, "Yes."

Finding Hope in Rehab--February 23, 2011

> "They tried to make me go to rehab but I said 'no, no, no'"
> --Amy Winehouse, Rehab (2007)

She sat in my office, a mother worn out from caring, emotionally drained, sharing her pain of a son who had been in and out, in and out of drug rehab. Now he had left rehab again. And she didn't know what to do.

It's a problem that's affecting more and more families. I could trot out statistic after statistic to prove what we already know: alcohol and drug abuse is a real problem no matter where you live. A friend of mine, a local police officer, tells me the increase in drug usage during the last ten years in our town, Lebanon, Ky., is, in his words, "unbelievable." His statement could be echoed by police officers in Anytown, U.S.A.

For the burdened mother who sat in my office, only one drug statistic mattered: the one that involved her son. When it's your son or daughter, husband or wife, it's one, that one. And that one hurts. Deeply.

Once that one, your one, steps into that world of drug and alcohol abuse, it's difficult to step out and stay out. Just ask Ted Williams, if you can find him. You remember Ted Williams, the homeless man with the golden voice who became an overnight sensation on Youtube? After being cleaned up, and fed, Ted's story of hope and second chances appeared on all the major news broadcasts. But Ted had a little problem that loomed ever so big: alcohol. According to his daughter, during Ted's sudden rise to fame, he "consumed at least a bottle of Gray Goose a night. That's not including the Coronas he ordered, that's not including the Budweisers he ordered, the other alcohol, the wines. He drinks heavily." But with the support and encouragement of Dr. Phil, Ted entered rehab, but is reported to have checked out only 12 days later. Let's hope the best for Ted, wherever he is. It's an uphill climb. Celebrity status doesn't change the addiction within.

Charlie Sheen should know it, even if he hasn't hit bottom yet. Sheen, as of 2010, was the highest paid actor on television, earning $1.8 million per episode for appearing on "Two and a Half Men." But Sheen's personal problems abound: Partying with reckless abandon landed him in rehab once again. A few days later, Sheen announced his decision to rehab in the comfort of his L.A. mansion. We wonder how seriously he is about rehab when he admitted to radio host Dan Patrick, "I was sober for five years a long time ago and was just bored out of my tree." Sheen then confessed, "It's inauthentic -- it's not who I am. I didn't drink for 12 years and, man, that first one, Dan. Wow." But Sheen knows the fragility of his condition. Addressing the producers of "Two and a Half Men," Sheen warned, "Check it. It's like, I heal really quickly. But I unravel pretty quickly. So get me right now, guys."

And there she sat, the broken hearted mother in my office, a mom with images of a son lost to an addiction and memories of an innocent little boy who played in the back yard, loved his guitar and four-wheeler. A good kid. Just like Ted Williams and Charlie Sheen, and thousands of others who have been sucked into a black hole of addiction, a hole where the drink or drug of choice drains life, dulls the senses, dissolves right from wrong, true from false, and once having destroyed a life, tosses its lifeless victim into the lap of grieving loved ones who are left to ask--"Where did we go wrong? What didn't we do?"--crying aloud like coyotes in the loneliness of the midnight air.

But even in despair there is hope. As one man tells it in the classic book, Alcoholics Anonymous, "I once knew a woman who was crying before a meeting. She was approached by a five-year-old girl who told her, 'You don't have to cry here. This is a good place. They took my daddy and they made him better.'"

Addiction is an illness. But there are treatments. And there is One who helps, never abandoning the distraught, the depressed, and, yes, the despised, the One who hears the humble prayer: "God, grant me the serenity to accept the things I cannot change, courage to change the things I can, and the wisdom to know the difference."

Discovering diamonds may be closer than you think--
September 25, 2011

"It's taken me a lifetime to get here, and I don't live that far," she said as we were walking toward the monastery, just before we passed the sign that says, "Silence beyond this point."

I was on the way back from someplace else when I had taken a slight detour so I could stop, just in time for the 2:15 p.m. prayer time (referred to by Cistercian monks as None) at the Abbey of Gethsemani in Trappist, Kentucky. She was stately looking, walking with an heir of relaxed formality, even though she was wearing kakis, a simple green pull-over, and sneakers. She looked to be about 60 to 65, but I had a feeling she was younger than her years.

She was responding to my question, "Are you on a retreat?" which she was, and before I could ask why it had taken her so long to get to Gethsemani or find out where she was from, we had slipped into the silence that draws so many to this place, Gethsemani.

As I was driving home a short time later, her statement stayed with me: "It's taken me a lifetime to get here, and I don't live that far."

We so often miss the treasures that are closest to home, don't we? Chances are, the happiness, fulfillment, and joy you are searching for are within the reach of your grasp right now. We spend a lifetime frantically searching the world over for whatever it is we are after, when the whole world is contained within every breath we breathe, if we would only pause long enough to embrace it in all the fullness of its time.

I'm reminded of the story Dr. Russell Conwell became famous for telling in the late 19th century, although the story didn't originate with him. It's the story about a man who lived in Africa during the days when diamond mines were being discovered there. A visitor told the farmer about the discovery of the mines, and the farmer became so enamored with the news the visitor shared, that the farmer sold his farm to search the African continent for diamonds. He spent the rest of his life in a futile effort to find diamonds.

Penniless and despondent, he finally threw himself into a river and drowned.

Meanwhile, the man who bought the farm stumbled across an unusual rock in a creek bed on the farm. He placed it on the mantel of his fireplace. Then the man who had told the first farmer about the discovery of diamonds in Africa came by once again. Seeing the stone on the mantel, he informed the farmer it wasn't any stone, it was a diamond--one of the largest ever. Upon investigating, they found the farm filled with them. One of the richest diamond mines in the world been discovered on the farm that the first man had sold to search for diamonds.

The point of the story of course is that we search for what we already have within us, at least potentially. We fail to enjoy the life we've been given because we don't examine the life we've been given.

How far do you have to travel before you can find happiness, peace, joy, contentment?

Having discovered the diamond mine within, we can make diamonds wherever we are.

A messy divorce results in a mother's determination to spend more time with her child, and a diamond is formed; a writer finds his voice while reading the works of a favorite author, and a diamond is discovered; a teacher gives possibilities to her students, and diamonds multiply.

It's often from obscure places--away from center stage--in difficult circumstances, somewhere south of Easy Street, that we discover the diamonds within. And whether they are recognized by others at the time is inconsequential, for diamonds will certainly shine with a brightness that lights up the heavens, illuminating the way for others, enlightening those encumbered with darkness, brightening the path of our own journey, a journey that is worth the pain, even though it may take a lifetime to get there.

Choose your destination carefully, you might just have to stay there--May 16, 2012

> *"Last thing I remember, I was*
> *Running for the door*
> *I had to find the passage back*
> *To the place I was before*
> *'Relax' said the night man,*
> *'We are programmed to receive.*
> *You can check-out any time you like,*
> *But you can never leave!'"*
> ---The Eagles, "Hotel California"

My cousins had picked me up at Love Field in Dallas, TX. I was to preside at their father's funeral the next day. After visiting with their family in their mother's home, they drove me to my hotel.

At least I thought it was my hotel.

They had taken care of my flight plans, and my dad said I could stay in the same hotel with him, my brother, sister-in-law, and nephew.

"It's the same hotel we stayed in last year when we were in Arlington, TX, for Brian's wedding," Dad emphasized.

My cousins remembered exactly where that hotel was located because they had visited us there when we in Arlington the year before.

"We'll see you at the church in the morning," they said as they left me at the hotel.

I tried to check in at the front desk. "I should have a room under the name of my father, L.D. Whitlock," I told the night clerk.

"No, we have no room under that name," she informed me.

I went down the list: my brother Mark, my nephew Brian, his wife, Mandy. There was no reservation under any of those names.

"Hmmm, I'll just call them," I told the night clerk.

"We're here, waiting on you, in room 231," Mark told me on my cell phone.

Relieved that I was in the right place, I made my way to the elevator and down the long hallway to room 231.

I knocked loudly on the door, proudly announcing my presence to my family.

And much to my surprise, a kind Oriental man opened the door.

I apologized. He smiled, bowed, and shut the door.

I'm now nonplussed and on my cell phone to my brother: "Don't you know your own room number, Nimrod?

Still on the phone, he asks his wife, Joy, to check the room number.

"231, the number's right here," I hear her say.

"That can't be right. I was just there and an Oriental man is in that room," I counter.

"What hotel are you at?" my brother asks.

"The same one as last year, just like Dad told me."

I now have to hold my cell phone away from my ear because my brother is howling with laughter. In fact, his son Brian told me later, Mark was on the floor in hysterics.

Somewhere in the planning process, they had changed hotels.

"How the heck was I supposed to know?" I demanded.

And I can still hear my dear ol' dad's explanation in the background, "Well, I thought someone would have told him."

Making my way back down the hallway to the elevator, and to the front desk, I can hear Don Henley and the Eagles singing, "Welcome to the Hotel California."

But alas, the night clerk, suppressing a snicker at my plight, happily pointed me to the front door, where I could wait on my not-so-compassionate big brother to pick me up.

And later, as I got in the van with him and my nephew Brian, I was glad to be leaving a place where I didn't belong. And I thought of how easy it had been to wind up in the wrong place.

Finding the place where you belong sometimes requires checking the sources, repeating directions, and making sure you have reliable information. It was C.S. Lewis who observed in his book, *The Screwtape Letters*, "The safest road to hell is the gradual one--the gentle slope, soft underfoot, without sudden turnings, without milestones, without signposts."

Finding life as it is supposed to be, as it is truly meant to be, is like a journey. And the search itself prompts questions like, "Where are you going?" And "Who are you, really?"

That life is discovered somewhere in the admission that only One has the answers to the questions of our deepest longings--desires only satisfied by living within the Eternal Now.

The late Eastern Orthodox priest and church historian, Fr. Alexander Schmemann aptly wrote, "Eternal life is not what begins after temporal life; it is the eternal presence of the totality of life." As we find our place in that life, we discover we've been holding the key unlocking the door to true freedom all along.

No, I don't want to stay one night in the Hotel Californian or any other place other than the place I was meant to be, a place where I can breathe in the fresh air of eternal life.

And enjoy the freedom of coming and going in the Eternal Presence forever.

When travelers find each other--April 11, 2012

My wife and I were the only customers in the souvenir and gift shop, lone shoppers during an off-season in Daytona Beach, Florida.

The lady at the cash register was kind but guarded, like the person checking your ID at airport security. But something about this lady intrigued me: Was she shy or resentful? Uncaring or prudent? Calloused or bruised?

Directing me to the next aisle, she snapped, staccato style, "Sweatshirts and hoodies over there; caps, next aisle." Her accent, which I guessed to be Eastern European, was heavy.

Rummaging through the sweatshirts, I found one I liked. "How do you think this one fits?" I asked, trying to draw her into a conversation.

"Da large, better. Medium, too small," she glowered at me over her reading glasses.

Feeling like a grade school student who had asked a question with an obvious answer yet still unconvinced of it, I was afraid to state my disagreement with her size assessment.

"Where are you from?" I cautiously queried, realizing the question was risky: I feared she would ignore me, refusing to reveal that much about herself, ceasing any possibility for further conversation.

"Europe," was her blunt response.

I plowed on: "Eastern Europe?"

"Greece."

"Oh, a beautiful country," I said, smiling. "I visited there many years ago. I loved all the historical sites in Athens--the Acropolis, the Pantheon."

My tourist resume drew no response. But I wasn't ready to give up, not yet.

"I studied Classical Greek in college. In fact, I majored in it."

Straight faced, she continued staring right through me as if I weren't there.

Unable to break the conversation code, I finally turned and walked away.

Three steps down the aisle, I turned back around.

"Someday I would like to visit the monastery at Mt. Athos," I blurted.

It was like I had said the magic word that opened a secret door; she now invited me in for a visit. Grinning, she looked directly at me: "Holy men of God are there."

Encouraged, I asked, "Are you Eastern Orthodox?"

"Ahh, yes, Eastern Orthodox," she nodded, as if I had mentioned a close personal friend.

"I often pray using the comboschini of the Orthodox faith," I continued, pulling my prayer rope from my pocket.

Smiling like her long awaited dinner guest had finally arrived to enjoy her gyros and baklava, she showed me her prayer rope and then turning around, opened a drawer and pulled out a picture album.

"You look," she commanded, opening the book for me: "Pictures of my home."

She was beaming now, pointing out photograph after photograph of her church, her town, its beaches, the mountains, the grandeur of her homeland.

I could imagine her carefully lifting the photo album from the drawer when no one was in the store and gazing into the pictures, slowly inhaling the fresh air of Greece.

"You miss your home?"

The tears in her eyes were her answer.

There is a common thread among us, connecting us to places so dissimilar and so alike. Sometimes, like travelers on the same road, we meet at the intersection of different faiths, and in their diverse expressions we find a commonality reminding us of familiar beginnings, a spiritual likeness that stays with us on the road to new discoveries.

Other times, we bump into each other on the entrance ramp of a shared place, a common culture, even though on that traveled, yellow bricked road, it's obvious we're no longer in Kansas anymore, for had we stayed where we were, never venturing to ask--Where? Who?--we wouldn't have noticed the other travelers. We're too familiar with them in Kansas.

Sometimes it's a prayer rope, or a holy book, or a religious symbol that jars our unconscious longings for traveling companions whose presence carries the scent of our spiritual origins and whose eyes squint toward our ultimate destination. And having waved bye as we travel on, we realize we have just met old friends for the first time.

Again.

But you have to look for them, or you'll swish by them--clerks at cash registers, waiters at restaurants, seat mates on airplanes--and they'll miss you, too, as casually as you pass strangers on opposite escalators.

And in those moments when we do pause to look, when we dare to inquire, we sometimes, even if only rarely, find ourselves sharing photographs of our mutual pilgrimage.

And along the long and winding road, those encounters can soothe the loneliness of the lonely, the bitterness of the bitter, the weariness of the weary.

Against her earlier recommendation, I bought the medium, not the large sweatshirt.

But my new friend didn't seem to notice.

She was too busy showing me her life journey in photographs.

www.ingramcontent.com/pod-product-compliance
Lightning Source LLC
Chambersburg PA
CBHW061603110426
42742CB00039B/2743